THE
CATAMARAN
BOOK

fernhurst
B O O K S

www.fernhurstbooks.co.uk

THE CATAMARAN BOOK

Brian Phipps

First published 1989, second edition 1992, third edition 1998

Fernhurst Books, Duke's Path, High Street, Arundel, West Sussex BN18 9AJ
Tel:01903 882277 Fax:01903 882715

ISBN 1 898660 44 1

Photographic credits
All photographs by John Woodward, with the exception of the following
Brian Phipps: pages 15 (pic 28); 16 (pics 29.30,33,34); 72
Yachting Photographics: pages 31,34 (bottom), 40,41,47, 59,61,63,67,76,77,78,85,87,91,92-3
Hobie Cat Europe SA: page 62 (bottom)
Chris Davies pages 96-128
Thanks to Windsport at Grafham Water for hosting the Hawk
shoot, and to Dave Graham for crewing.

Cover photo of the Hawk courtesy of The Laser Centre, the Dart courtesy
of Brian Phipps/Windsport, and the Hobie courtesy of Kos.

Acknowledgements
Few books are the product of just one person's achievements, and my thanks must go to all
the instructors at the Cat. Clinic for their help in developing the effective teaching systems that
we now use. I would also like to thank Lynn Fraser for the excellent crewing skills during the
photographic sessions. I personally shall miss the friendship and support of the late Kim Stephens,
who made a valuable contribution to the book and, as a long-standing catamaran sailor, helped me
and many others in our sailing careers. We will benefit from Kim's enthusiasm for catamaran sailing
for a long time to come.
Thank you Kim.

Brian Phipps

Designed by John Woodward and Creative Byte
Artwork by PanTek and Creative Byte
Printed in China through World Print

Contents

Introduction

Why do people sail catamarans? Is it their speed? Is it their power? Is it their shape? Is it their size? By the time you have finished this book I hope you will understand just why people do sail cats and how you can safely join this fast-moving and exciting form of sailing. The book is arranged in four parts:

Part One shows the beginner how to understand the wind, how to rig the boat and how to enjoy his first sail – and get back to the beach safely! It explains all aspects of catamaran sailing in winds between force 2 and 3. I suggest that experienced sailors browse through this section and make notes of the subtle differences between catamaran and monohull sailing.

Part Two contains information for those who can already sail and those who have successfully completed Part One. It covers light and strong wind techniques, trapezing, downwind sailing and sailing on the sea. You will gain an insight into handling your cat in adverse conditions, so that when you are out sailing in strong winds the potential speed will be thrilling rather than frightening, and light winds will be rewarding rather than frustrating.

Part Three is an introduction to the main aspects of racing, with the emphasis on how to get the best out of your boat and improve your position in a race. Catamarans are fast, situations change rapidly and advantages can be won and lost quickly, so you must try to stay on top of each situation if you want to finish near the front of the fleet.

Part Four covers even more advanced skills. Many modern cats are fitted with a gennaker (an asymmetric spinnaker), and we look in detail at how to handle these exciting downwind sails in all wind conditions. Go for the wild thing! To counteract the extra leverage, twin trapezes have been introduced and we cover helming from the wire, a slightly different skill from crewing on the trapeze.

Finally, in case it all goes wrong, we show how to recover from a capsize with the gennaker up.

Whatever you experience in sailing, welcome to the fleet that has three things in common:

SPEED.....POWER.....AND TWO HULLS!

PART ONE:

GETTING STARTED

Which catamaran?

There are many different types of catamaran. They vary in hull shape and sail plan, and some have centreboards while others have skegs or even assymmetric hulls. Whichever type you choose the basic sailing techniques and concepts are the same; the important thing is that your cat does the job you want.

Don't just take the salesman's word for it –take a trial sail, talk to other catamaran sailors, find out about class associations and second-hand values. It is important that the boat fits your personal needs as well as your pocket! There is no point buying an all-out racing machine if you simply want to club race or cruise.

Capsizing and tacking a catamaran are probably the main concerns of the beginner. In fact a well-designed catamaran is easily righted and a demonstration capsize on your trial sail will help allay your fears and show what the boat will do. You should also make sure you can tack the cat through the wind. In short, just like anything else, try before you buy, then you will not be disappointed.

HULL SHAPE

The choice of hull shape depends on your requirements. All hull shapes will perform adequately in a wide range of conditions, but excel in probably only one or two.

Hulls with centreboards
Catamarans fitted with daggerboards or centreboards are generally the most efficient upwind, especially in light airs. They do, however, require maintenance, and must be handled carefully when launching and beaching. You must also avoid underwater obstructions. When daggerboards are raised they stick up out of the hull, and it hurts if you are thrown against one of them. Pivoting centreboards fold up into a centreboard box inside the hull. This provides a very neat housing and does away with the injury problem, but you must take care to prevent stones and sand getting into the box itself when beaching, as this will restrict the movement of the centreboards and can cause internal damage.

Asymmetric hulls
Asymmetric hulls are designed to replace daggerboards or centreboards. Each hull is handed – that is the port hull is a mirror image of the starboard hull. Although not generally as efficient as hulls with centreboards, assymmetric hulls do simplify the layout of the catamaran, making it easier to handle.

The amount of rocker (curve) built into the hull

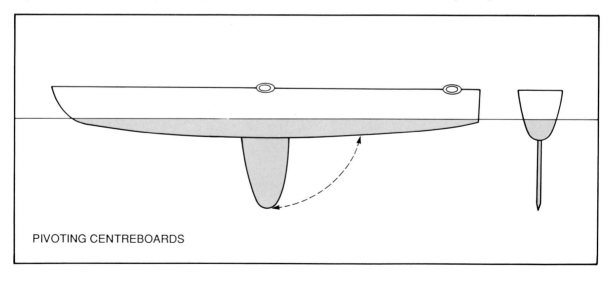

PIVOTING CENTREBOARDS

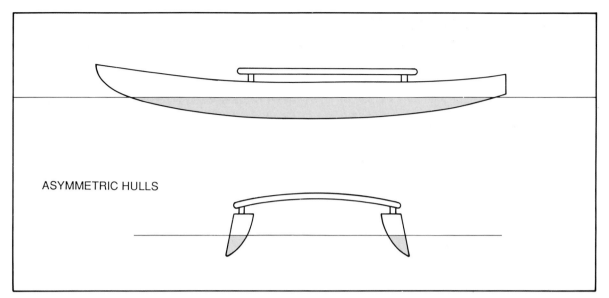

ASYMMETRIC HULLS

also affects its performance: with more rocker the catamaran will surf better, but with less rocker the performance in flat and choppy sea conditions improves.

Hulls with skegs

The 'skeg' design also does away with the need for centreboards. Each hull is identical in shape, and sideways movement through the water is restricted by a deep keel that forms a skeg about two-thirds of the way down the hull.

Well suited to both flat water and sea conditions, the skeg system is often seen in European-designed catamarans.

SAIL DESIGN AND SHAPE

The vast majority of catamarans have fully battened mainsails and high-ratio jibs for maximum efficiency.

Some mainsails are supported along the foot by a boom; others are loose-footed, with no boom. A boom allows the mainsail shape to be adjusted easily using sail foot tension, kicking strap tension and mainsheet tension. A loose-footed sail simplifies the system and does away with the potentially dangerous boom; sail shape and position are controlled by the mainsheet sheeting angle and tension.

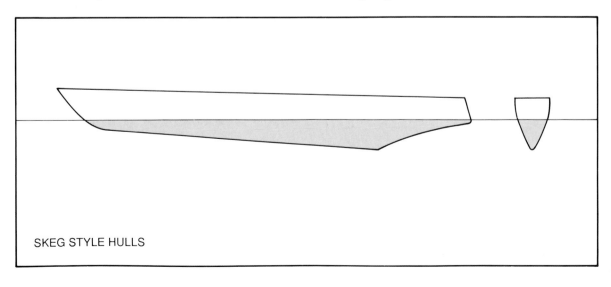

SKEG STYLE HULLS

Parts of the boat

GLOSSARY

Aft: towards the back of the boat.
Bow: the foremost end of the boat.
Burgee: a flag normally flown from the top of a mast.
Batten: a thin plastic strip which fits into a long narrow pocket in the sail.
Bridle wire: one of the two wires connected to the bow and forestay on a catamaran.
Clew: the lower after-most corner of a sail.
Foot: the bottom edge of a sail.
Forward: towards the bows of a boat.
Forestay: the wire supporting the mast in a fore and aft direction.
Gunwhale: the outermost edge of the craft.
Head: the top corner of a sail.
Hounds: the connecting point on the mast for rigging that gives it support.
Halyard: a rope or wire used to hoist or lower sails.
Jib sheet: the rope used to control the position of the jib when under sail.
Leech: the trailing edge of a sail.
Leeward: the side of the boat on which the mainsail is set when sailing.
Luff: the front edge of a sail.
Mainsheet: the rope controlling the position of the mainsail.
Mast heel: the casting at the base of the mast.
Port: the left-hand side of a craft looking forward.
Shroud: a wire securing the mast in position and preventing it from falling sideways.
Shackle: a 'U' shaped piece of metal secured with a pin, used for securing halyards to sails etc.
Starboard: the right-hand side of a craft looking forward.
Stern: the aft-most area of a boat.
Tack: the lower forward corner of a sail.
Tiller: a length of aluminium which fits into the rudder head to allow steerage.
Tiller extension: a length of aluminium connected to the tiller by a universal joint which allows steerage while leaning out.
Trapeze wire: a wire used to extend the body beyond the gunwhale of the boat.
Transom: the flat area across the back of the boat to which the rudder is hung.
Windward: the side of the boat opposite to which the mainsail is set when sailing.

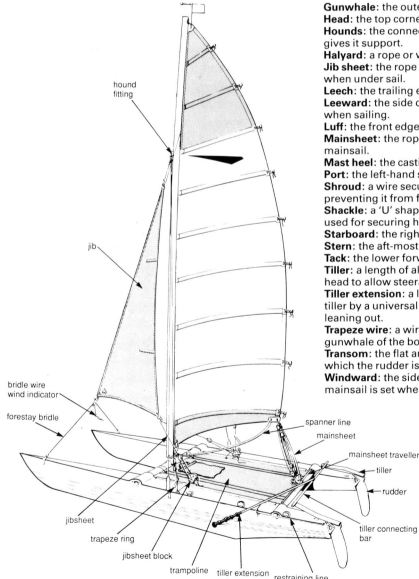

hound fitting

jib

bridle wire
wind indicator

forestay bridle

spanner line

mainsheet

mainsheet traveller

tiller

rudder

jibsheet

trapeze ring

jibsheet block

trampoline   tiller extension   restraining line

tiller connecting bar

The hulls

Remember that catamaran hulls can be left-handed, right-handed or identical, depending on the design. Today most hulls are made of G.R.P., and some small catamarans are even made of polypropylene. Each hull is a sealed unit, but it has built-in buoyancy to keep it afloat if it is damaged. A small hole positioned in a suitable dry place allows the hull to 'breathe' and stops it expanding or contracting. All fittings connected to the hull should be sealed to stop water seepage and should be vibration resistant.

Mainsail/jib

It is advisable to roll the sails when they are not in use, and de-tension the battens for storage. This will prolong the life of the sails and reduce fabric stretch. Rinsing down with fresh water is also advisable, although not always possible.

Mainsail downhaul

The mainsail downhaul is the control line that puts power into the sail. You will notice that with no tension on the luff (the front edge of the sail), the mainsail has little shape and is rather like a flat piece of cardboard. When the downhaul is tensioned the sail is forced into shape and develops power.

Spanner line

The spanner line is normally connected to the foot of the mainsail or boom and to the bottom of the mast. It is adjusted to control the amount of mast rotation for the best airflow over the mainsail: a loose spanner line allows a lot of rotation, while a tight spanner line restricts it.

Jib and mainsail halyards

The halyards are the lines that hoist the sails. They often have halyard locks incorporated, as described later in the book.

Shrouds, forestay and bridle wires

These are the wires that hold the mast upright. They are subjected to incredible stress and should be checked regularly for any sign of corrosion or wear.

Trapeze wires

The job of a trapeze wire is to support the crew (or helmsman) when he extends his body weight outboard by 'standing' on the edge of the hull.

The wires are connected to the mast about two-thirds of the way up and run down almost parallel to the shrouds. They each have a large stainless steel ring at the bottom that clips into the crew's harness, and are loosely connected to the boat by shock-cord. They can be adjusted to support the crew at the correct trapezing height.

Trapeze restraining line

The restraining lines are connected to the transom of the boat and can be hooked into the ring at the end of the trapeze wire. They are mainly used for reaching in strong winds since they help the crew stay back and prevent his being thrown forward.

Rudder and tiller assembly

The rudders are normally fixed in the raised position when on the beach and then lowered when the boat is on the water. The tiller arms are joined by a connecting bar which is controlled by the tiller extension. The tiller extension is your steering wheel and you must hang on to it all the time when you are sailing.

Mainsheet, jibsheet and traveller line

These are the ropes that control the positions of the sails. The helm and crew should be able to adjust these at any time to allow for changes in wind strength or direction, just as you would do with the accelerator and brake pedal in a car.

Trampoline and toestraps

The trampoline covers the area between the hulls to allow easy movement from one hull to the other. The toestraps lie along the trampoline and secure your feet when you are leaning out over the side of the hull. As your crew becomes more proficient he will use the trapeze, and secure his feet in the toe loops on the side of the hull.

Main and rear beams

These are the spars that hold the two hulls together. They must be securely fastened and in good condition.

Mast and mast ball

The mast ball allows the mast to rotate about its axis, giving improved airflow over the sails. The mast itself is normally sealed, giving a degree of buoyancy that helps prevent the boat turning over completely if you capsize.

Putting the boat together

Assuming your boat has been delivered as two hulls, a mast and a box of equipment, first lay out the various parts and identify them. Then:

1 Position the hulls side by side, about three metres apart on level ground. Take the main beam and rear beam (or in some cases the trampoline frame) and connect them securely to one hull. Swivel the remaining hull into position and slide it onto the free ends of the beams, keeping the hulls in line during the process.

2 Feed the trampoline into the track on the main beam and along the insides of the hulls. Then lace up the trampoline as tightly as possible at the rear beam. Remember that the trampoline will stretch during use and need retensioning at a later date.

3 Lay the heel of the mast onto the mast ball with the mast raked aft and secure the heel – usually with a pin. This stops the heel jumping off while the mast is being swung into the upright position.

1 Having aligned the hulls three metres apart, insert the main beam with the ball facing up.

2 Push the beam right home to the thrust pad.

3 Insert the rear beam with the traveller facing up.

4 Push the beams into the other hull.

5 Make sure the clip is located correctly.

4 Connect the hound fitting and standing rigging. Untangle the shroud wires and connect them to the shroud plates, making sure there are no kinks or twists in the wires.

5 Secure the bridle wires to the bow plates and lay the forestay and trapeze wires out towards the bow. Feed the main and jib halyards through their sheaves and rings ready for hoisting the sails.

6 You are now ready to raise the mast. One person guides the mast forward from the back of the boat while the other person stands in front of the main beam and pulls the weight of the mast forward, using the trapeze handles or forestay and walking backwards slowly towards the bow of the boat. As the mast is guided into the upright position the rear helper steps up onto the trampoline and continues to guide the mast until the shroud wires come tight.

7 Connect the forestay to the bridle wires with a shackle or lanyard. When all is secure the mast pin can be removed and the trapeze wires attached to their shockcords.

8 Attach the mainsheet, jibsheets, traveller line, toestraps, trapeze restrainer lines, 'O' rings, hatch covers, rudders, tiller connecting bar and tiller extension.

9 It is a good idea at this point to familiarise yourself with the various positions and adjustments available on your boat: the mainsheet and jibsheet jamming blocks, the toestrap positions and, most important of all, the method of raising and lowering the rudders (and centreboards, if you have them).

6 Put on the rubber sealing rings and the hatch covers.

7 Feed the trampoline into the track in the main beam.

8 Slide the trampoline into the tracks on the hulls.

9 Insert the trampoline tube.

10 Lace the trampoline tube to the rear beam . . .

. . . running the lacing through the fittings as shown.

11 Tension the lacing.

12 Stretch the trampoline.

13 Tension the lacing again and tie it.

14 Put on the toe straps.

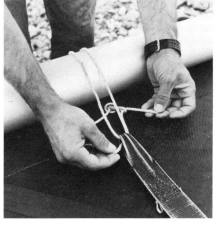
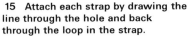

15 Attach each strap by drawing the line through the hole and back through the loop in the strap.

16 Draw the free end of the line through the loop in the other end and tie it securely.

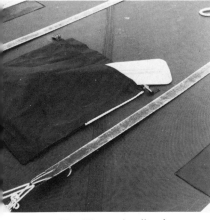

17 Clip on the ditty bag and put in the paddle.

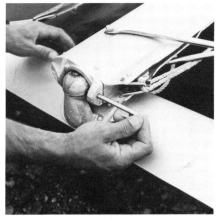

18 Push the mast foot onto the ball and insert the retaining pin.

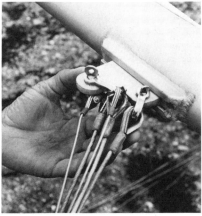

19 Connect the hound fitting the right way up.

20 Push the jib halyard through the locking ring.

21 Connect the shrouds to the shroud plates on the hulls.

22 Set up the forestay bridle.

23 Make sure the halyards are properly attached, then raise the mast by pulling on the trapeze wires.

24 Shackle the forestay to the bridle.

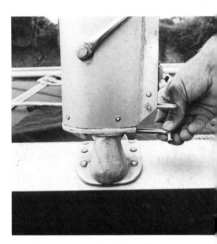

25 Remove the retaining pin.

26 Clip the trapeze ring to the shockcord.

27 Rig the restraining line.

28 Attach the jib blocks and reeve the jib sheets.

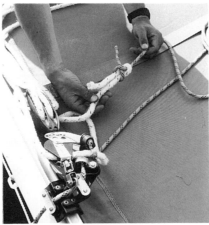
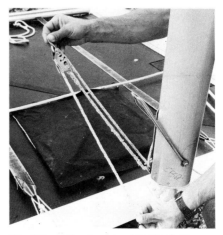

29 Attach the mainsheet to the traveller.

30 Tie the end of the mainsheet to the traveller line using a sheet bend.

31 Attach the downhaul to the foot of the mast.

32 Attach the rudders, making sure the retaining clips are operating.

33 Fix the connecting bar to the tillers.

34 Attach the tiller extension to the connecting bar.

35 Slip the battens into the mainsail and tie them.

36 Push the loose ends into the batten pockets.

37 Test the tension by 'popping' the battens.

HOISTING THE SAILS

Most catamarans are moved on a simple trolley placed under the hulls at the balance point. The bows then serve as a 'handle' and the cat can be moved easily and efficiently. Before hoisting the sails move the boat close to the water with the bows pointing into the wind. Protect the keel of each hull and slide the trolley out forward to make the catamaran secure, ready for hoisting the sails.

Raising the mainsail
1 Tension the battens in the mainsail, so that they just flick from one side to the other.
2 Shackle the main halyard to the head of the mainsail, making sure that the knot is facing aft so that on hoisting, the mast lock at the top of the mast engages the ring. Most catamarans have their sails secured at the top of the mast to reduce halyard stretch.
3 Feed the luff of the mainsail into the mast luff groove, and hoist.
4 Connect the downhaul, but do not tension it at this stage. Tensioning the luff creates a wing shape in the sail and will make the boat try to sail away – which you don't want while you're still on the beach!
5 Connect the spanner line and vang (kicking strap), but not the mainsheet.

Raising the jib
1 Attach the jib halyard to the head of the sail with the open part of the hook facing aft and hoist the jib so the hook engages the ring.
2 Tension the jib luff downhaul carefully: it should be slightly slacker than the forestay wire.
3 Finally connect the jibsheets.

38 Attach the main halyard with the knot at the back.

39 Pull up the mainsail until it locks at the top.

40 The ring will have slipped over the locking hook at the masthead.

41 Feed the bottom of the mainsail luff into the foot of the mast.

42 Attach the spanner line to the mast fitting.

43 Attach the downhaul to the sail, but do not tighten it.

♠   Attach the jib halyard with the hook at the back.

♠   Pull up the jib, attaching the hanks as you go.

♠   With the jib right up, pull the clew to fix the hook onto the ring.

♠   Attach the jib sheets to the clew of the jib.

♠   Secure the tack of the jib to the jib downhaul.

♠   Tie the jib downhaul, adjusting the tension to suit the wind (see p.81).

BOAT TOGETHER CHECKLIST

- Rudder fitted correctly
- Control lines free, and not tangled
- No kinks in wire
- All split rings taped
- All shackles done up tight
- Trampoline tight
- Sail battens tensioned
- Sail halyard locks in operation
- Hatch covers secure

A touch of theory

A sailing craft is rather like a car: it requires fuel and an engine. In the case of a sailing boat the fuel is the wind and the engine is the sails. The stronger the wind the more power is produced from the sails and the faster the boat will go . . . providing you do not lose control and capsize!

The forward motion is produced by the flow of moving air over the sails, from front to back. Air flowing over the windward side of each sail causes pressure whilst air flowing over the leeward side causes suction. The resulting force is in the direction of arrows A and B in the diagram and is at right angles to each sail.

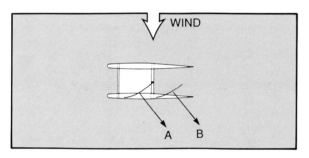

This force pushes the boat forward and sideways. The forward motion propels the boat towards its goal and the sideways force is resisted by the water pressure on the skeg-shaped hull or centreboard.

The weight of the helmsman and crew on the windward side counteracts the heeling (capsize) effect. The stronger the wind the more the catamaran wants to heel over and the further out the crew must lean. Eventually a point is reached where, to produce more power, the crew must trapeze on the side of the hull. Alternatively

the helmsman can let the sail out a bit and spill some wind, but this will reduce the power and normally make the cat slow down.

When sailing against the wind the sails are pulled right in and the forces A and B are at near right-angles to the boat. The sideways force is now at its strongest, so you need full extension of the centreboards or maximum use of the skegs to stop the boat going sideways.

When sailing with the wind coming from behind the sails are let out and the force is now pushing directly the way the boat wants to move, so no centreboard is needed and the skegs have no function.

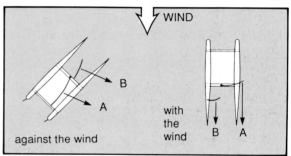

How can I steer?

When a cat is sailing straight the water flows past the rudders undisturbed. When the rudders are turned, the water is deflected. The water hitting the rudders pushes them, and the back of the boat, in direction C. The bows turn to the left.

In short, pulling the tiller extension towards you turns the bows away from you, and vice versa. Note that the rudders work only when the cat is moving, and water is flowing past them.

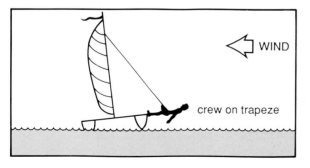

crew on trapeze

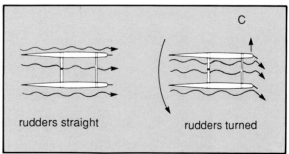

rudders straight   rudders turned

How can I stop?

It is the wind in the sails that makes the boat go forward. To stop the cat, take the wind out of the sails either by letting out the sheets, or by altering course gently towards the wind. In a cat it is best to slow down but not quite stop, since if you stop you will be unable to steer.

How can I tell which way the wind is blowing?

Everything in sailing is related to wind direction. You can tell which way the wind is blowing by the feel of it on your cheek, by the wave direction or by using a burgee. Remember, the burgee points to the way the wind is going.

POINTS OF SAILING

Look at the diagram on the opposite page. There are three points of sailing:

Reaching – the boat sails *across* the wind.
Beating – the boat sails *towards* the wind.
Running – the boat sails with the wind *behind* it.

Reaching

When reaching, the boat sails at right angles to the wind, which is blowing from behind your back. The sails should be about halfway out and the centreboards, if fitted, should be about halfway up.

Beating

If you want to change course towards the wind, you must push the centreboard down and pull in the sails as you turn. You can go on turning towards the wind until the sails are pulled right in. Then you are *beating*.

If you try to turn further towards the wind you enter the 'no-go area'. The sails flap and the boat stops.

If you want to reach a point that is upwind of your current position you have to *beat* zigzag fashion, as shown in the diagram.

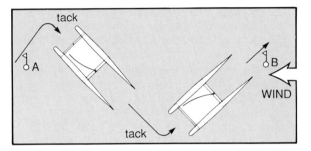

At the end of each 'zig' the boat turns through an angle of 90°. This is called a *tack*. The boat turns 'through' the wind – the sails blow across to the other side and the crew must shift their weight across the boat to balance it.

Running

From a reach, you may want to change course away from the wind. Pull up the centreboards if you have them and let out the sails as you turn. You can go on turning until the wind is coming from behind the boat. Then you are *running*.

If you turn more, the boat will *gybe*. The wind blows from the other side of the boat and you must shift your weight across to balance it.

⬥ Reaching   ⬥ Beating   ⬥ Running

WIND

NO-GO AREA

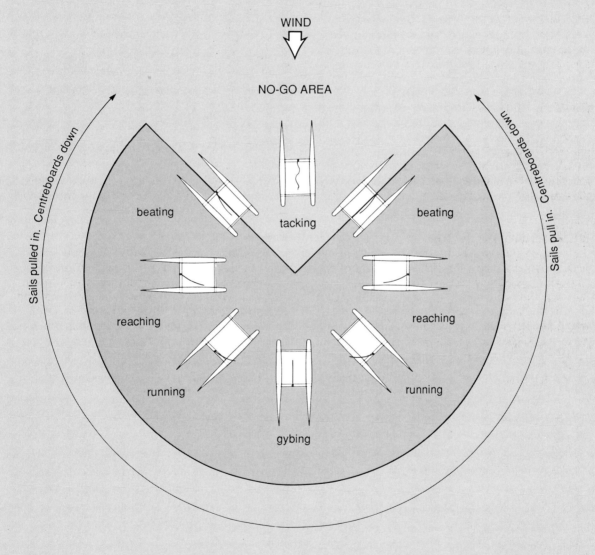

beating   tacking   beating

reaching   reaching

running   gybing   running

Sails pulled in. Centreboards down

Sails pull in. Centreboards down

Your first sail

CLOTHING

You can wear the same clothes for cat sailing as you would for dinghy sailing, including (and this is essential) a lifejacket or buoyancy aid, whatever the conditions. You will need a one-piece or two-piece wetsuit plus a spray suit on top and sailing shoes and gloves. Even if the conditions look perfect it is best to take this minimum of clothing with you, for we all know how quickly conditions change. A hat is a good idea in extreme conditions, and as your confidence and ability increase you will need a trapeze harness. If you are the type who feels the cold, add extra sweaters under your spray-suit or consider a drysuit with thermal suit underneath. If you are cold and wet, sailing will not be as much fun as if you are warm and comfortable.

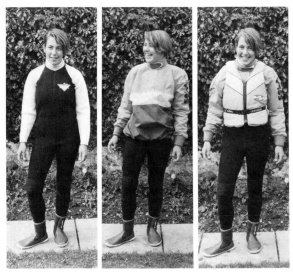

◆ Stay warm, comfortable and safe by wearing a wet suit, waterproof spray suit or jacket, and a buoyancy aid or lifejacket.

LAUNCHING

1 Choose a launch area with a cross-shore wind and clear sea access.
2 Push the trolley back under the balance point of your boat and move the catamaran into the water, keeping the bows within 45 degrees of the wind so the sails do not fill.
3 While the crew keeps the boat clear of the beach by holding the bridle wires and the bow, the helmsman takes the trolley ashore.
4 The helmsman connects the mainsheet, lowers the rudders halfway, tensions the mainsail luff downhaul and (for your first sail) sets the traveller in the centre of the beam. He also checks that the jib and mainsheet are free.

◆ Push the cat into the water at 45° to the wind.

◆ Hold the boat head-to-wind and remove the trolley.

◆ Connect the mainsheet and centre the traveller.

CHECKLIST BEFORE LEAVING BEACH

- Wind conditions: cross-shore, force 2-3
- Sensible clothing: buoyancy aid, wetsuit
- You understand the parts of the boat and their jobs
- You know the sequence of tacking (see page 42)
- The area off the beach is clear

Having checked the area immediately off the beach the helmsman positions himself on the windward side of the boat with the tiller in the hand nearest the stern and mainsheet in the forward hand, the rudders semi-raised and a small area of centreboard down (if fitted). The crew pushes the bows to a position across the wind and at the same time moves along the side of the boat to climb aboard forward of the shroud.

Sail away from the beach slowly, using the mainsheet as the accelerator. Once into deep water ease the mainsheet and lower the rudders (and centreboards if fitted) into their sailing positions. Until this point the boat is only under partial control and *must* be sailed slowly.

You are now ready to enjoy your first sail. Choose a goal across the wind, sheet in the mainsail until the telltales at the top of the sail are streaming, and go!

☛ Lower the rudders halfway.

☛ Tension the main downhaul.

☛ Crew pushes off and climbs on.

Because a catamaran goes quite fast it is important that you keep an eye out to see where you are going. As in a car you spend most of your time looking forward, with occasional glances at the set of the sails and the other boat controls. It is very easy to get involved in looking at the sails and sorting out the ropes, and not look where you are going – with embarrassing and sometimes expensive consequences.

SAILING POSITION

Everyone has their own individual way of sailing a boat, but it is a good idea to start from a position that has been proven. This is especially true of cat sailing where good technique will allow you to concentrate on other areas such as boatspeed and race tactics.

If you are the helmsman, you should steer with the tiller over your shoulder, your back hand holding it in a dagger grip. Your front hand is for constant adjustment of the mainsheet. This allows you to lean out easily, trap the mainsheet in your tiller hand when pulling in more mainsheet, and make controlled alterations of the traveller line. It is also a good idea to keep all excess control lines between your legs, to stop them being washed overboard.

If you are crewing, you should generally hold the jib sheet in your back hand unless trapezing off the stern quarter of the boat. Your front hand is used for adjusting the trapeze height.

Here you see two catamarans being sailed in slightly different windstrengths.

Medium winds
● The helmsman is sitting on the deck of the windward hull with his feet under the toestraps.
● The tiller is held in his back hand in a dagger grip, while the mainsheet is controlled by the forward hand.
● The crew is also positioned on the windward side but has her bottom over the edge of the gunwhale with her feet under the toestraps and the jibsheet held in her back hand. Should the wind become lighter the crew will need to move her weight towards the centreline of the boat, and if necessary to leeward, to keep the boat level.

Stronger winds
The wind has become a little stronger.
● The helmsman has moved his bottom over the gunwhale to sit out further and to help keep him in a stable position in the boat.
● The crew is giving extra leverage by using the trapeze wire with her feet on the gunwhale. To do this she needs to wear a trapeze harness to which the trapeze wire is hooked.

In sailing towards your goal across the wind try and keep the hulls 'tuned' correctly fore-and-aft by moving your weight forward or back to keep the waterline parallel to the water. Lean in or out and trim the sheets to keep the windward hull just kissing the water. Good hull and sail trim will give the boat a good turn of speed *and* make it easy to control.

As you approach your goal you will need to turn the boat round. You can do this by turning to the left or to the right, but at first you should turn

➥ **Medium-wind position, with both helm and crew on the trampoline.**

➥ **Strong-wind position, with the crew on the wire and the helm hiked out.**

● To tack, push the tiller away . . .   ● Steer through the wind . . .   ● And sail off.

it so the bows point first towards the wind, and then back to where you have sailed from: this turn is called a *tack*.

YOUR FIRST TACK

Get the boat into position ready for tacking by sailing as close to the wind as possible. To do this, pull the sails in tight, push the tiller extension away from you and point the bows towards the wind. When you reach the point where the jib is about to flap at the front (the luff) you will know that the boat is entering the 'no-go zone' and it will begin to slow down. Sail on the edge of the no-go zone for a while to keep up your speed.

Check that the area to windward is clear and initiate the tack. Push the tiller away from you

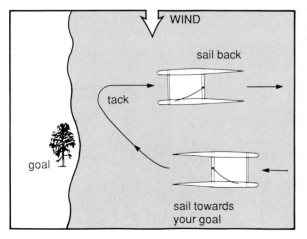

WIND

sail back

tack

goal

sail towards
your goal

and hold it there until the boat has passed through the no-go zone and is sailing on the new tack, with the wind in the other side of the sails. During this process you should both move to the other side of the boat, and at the end of the manoeuvre the crew lets off the 'old' jibsheet and pulls in the new one. Tacking is described in more detail on page 42.

Now head back to your original starting point. To get the boat sailing across the wind, pull the tiller extension towards you and ease the sails out until the jib is just about to flap and the telltales on either side of the mainsail (at the top) are flowing.

If you feel the boat is going too fast or you start to lose control, ease out the mainsheet and the jibsheet to slow down, but keep the boat heading across the wind towards your goal. When you get close to your starting point repeat the procedure of tacking through the no-go zone, and sail back out to your original goal. Remember that, before tacking, you must first sail the boat as close to the wind as possible. Make sure that during this exercise you are well clear of other craft and the shore.

If the boat for any reason does not complete the tack – that is, does not turn through 90° –you will have to get the boat sailing fast again before you make a second attempt.

Getting 'out of irons'
There are various reasons why a beginner may not complete a successful tack and these are listed on page 45. One major fault is not having the sails in tight as the boat turns into the tack,

so the boat does not even reach head-to-wind. The symptom of this is the bow being blown back onto its original course.

If, however, the boat reaches head-to-wind but there is insufficient boatspeed to complete the tack the boat will start to sail backwards. If this happens:

1   Keep the jib in on the original side to help blow the bow round.

2   Ease the mainsheet.

3   As the boat drifts backwards reverse the rudders to turn the boat onto its new heading.

4   Release the jib, pull in the mainsheet and the new jibsheet, and steer off in the direction you want to go.

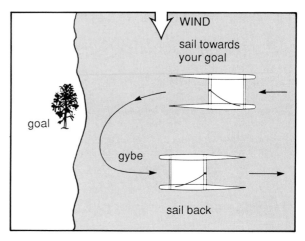

Gybing

Once you have mastered the art of tacking, try doing the opposite manoeuvre. Reach across the wind towards your goal, but this time instead of turning the boat towards the wind, turn it away from the wind. This is called a *gybe*.

Turn the boat from the reach by pulling the tiller extension towards you and, at the same time, let out the sails and the traveller. Watch the bridle wire wind indicator and keep turning until the indicator is 90° across the boat – you are now sailing downwind.

If the boat is turned further downwind the sails will stall and the boat will slow down considerably. The wind indicator will indicate this by blowing further forward than 90° across the boat. Prepare to gybe, as explained on page 54 – but first make sure you have sufficient sea room for the manoeuvre.

Once you have completed your gybe do not forget to check where you are going, then reset the traveller to the centre of the boat and set the mainsail and jib so that the telltales are flowing on the sails.

In force 2 to 3 you may consider gybing an easy option to tacking but it is important that you can do both, with ease and fluency, in strong and light winds – so practise.

To gybe, steer away from the wind . . .　　*Help the sail flip over . . .*　　*And sail off.*

C.A.T.

During the rest of the book we will be referring to the term **C.A.T.**
C = Crew weight and position, fore-and-aft, inboard and outboard.
A = Airflow – the position of the sails to give optimum performance.
T = Technique – how best to sail the boat given the sea, wind, tides and the movement of other craft.
C.A.T. is relevant to all points of sailing and worth remembering when you are on the water.

SAILING A SQUARE COURSE

The reach

Let's start off on a reach, with the traveller centred. (At a later stage we can use the traveller more effectively to improve the boat's performance.) Sail across the wind towards your goal.

C: Crew weight The boat should be balanced equally on each hull, and with the fore-and-aft trim adjusted so that the boat is level in the water. It is a good tip to look at the transom to see if it is dragging. If a gust of wind comes along and the boat accelerates be prepared to move your weight back to compensate for the downward pressure on the bows.

♣　Try to keep the boat flat and level on the water.

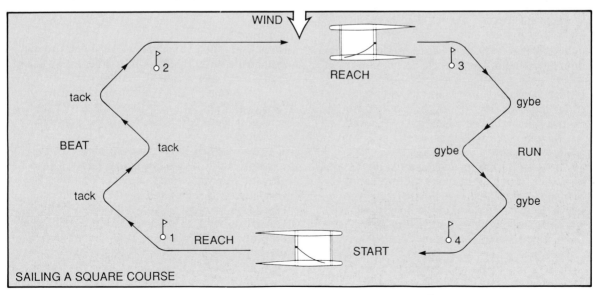

SAILING A SQUARE COURSE

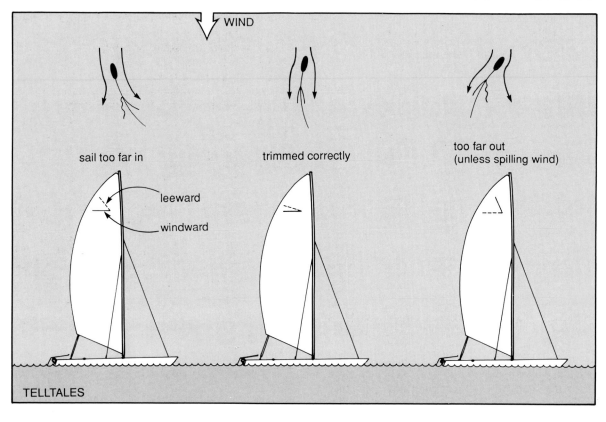

WIND

sail too far in   trimmed correctly   too far out
                                                     (unless spilling wind)

leeward

windward

TELLTALES

A: Airflow When setting the sails it is important to stop the sails flapping first, then 'fine tune' them using the telltales.

Telltales, sometimes called woollies or sail streamers, are simply threads of wool attached to the sails to show clearly the effect of the air passing over them. Their job is to help the helmsman or crew read the sails more clearly.

The telltales on both sides of each sail should constantly stream backwards, demonstrating a smooth passage of air over both surfaces.

If the leeward telltale starts to fall or circle, the air flowing over this side of the sail is disturbed and the sail should be eased out.

If the windward telltale stalls the sail should be pulled in to smooth the airflow.

In the case of the mainsail, you should start by using the mainsheet to make the top set of telltales react correctly. As you improve you will be able to make the majority of lower telltales flow correctly too by using the mainsheet, vang (kicking strap), batten tension and traveller position.

The jib can also be sheeted for maximum efficiency using its telltales as a guide.

T: Technique Try to keep looking forward, and allow for any tide or sideways drift. If the boat starts to lift a hull out of the water move your body weight outboard and if necessary ease the mainsail. If you have centreboards they should be positioned half way down.

The beat
When you reach your goal you will need to sail against the wind by *beating*, that is, zig-zagging your way to a new goal to windward.

Pull the sails in and push the rudders away from you. This will turn the boat towards the wind and allow you to start your progress to windward.

C: Crew weight Keep the boat balanced by moving your crew weight inboard and outboard. Trim the boat by positioning your combined crew weight so that the boat is level: normally you will have to be further forward than when reaching.

A: Airflow With the sails pulled in tight, point the boat towards the wind until the windward telltale on the jib begins to stall. At this point back off a few degrees to keep the boat sailing as close to the wind as possible.

↑ When you are beating the sideways force on the boat is tremendous, and the crew may need to go out on the trapeze to stop it heeling over too far.

T: Technique When sailing against the wind concentrate on sailing the fine line between entering the no-go zone and pointing too far away from the wind. You will have to make the decision when to tack and sail on the other side of the no-go zone to reach your goal – normally this new course is at about 90° to your previous heading.

If you have centreboards they will need to be right down on this point of sailing.

When you get to your windward goal you can relax and go back to a reach, as discussed above. Don't forget to pull your centreboards (if fitted) halfway up and use C.A.T. to get the most from your craft.

The run
After your next goal you will need to complete your square course by sailing downwind.

You can sail with the wind directly behind you in all catamarans but it is usually faster to zig-zag downwind. We will look at this technique in more detail on page 49.

C: Crew weight Make sure the boat is balanced evenly, and move aft so the bottoms of the transoms are only just out of the water.

A: Airflow Let the traveller right out to reduce sail twist. Ease the mainsail until it is just touching the shrouds and then let the jib out as much as possible without the telltales stalling.

You may find it easier with the crew on the leeward side of the boat.

T: Technique You may decide to sail straight downwind to begin with, but you will soon learn that it is quicker to zig-zag, keeping the sails at 90° to the *apparent* wind. To do this just keep an eye on the wind indicator between the bridle wires and concentrate on keeping it at 90° to the boat. When you gybe you will head off at 90° to your previous course. If you have centreboards raise them fully.

HEAVING TO

'Heaving-to' is something you can do if you:
● Need a rest!
● Need to stop to adjust something.
● Find yourself in a position where sailing could be dangerous.

The effect is to depower the sails and get them to balance each other out so that the boat simply drifts slowly sideways downwind. To to this on a catamaran:

1 Ease off the mainsheet and traveller line.
2 Pull the jib to the wrong side of the boat (the windward side) using the windward jibsheet.
3 Push the rudders over so that they try to point the boat into the wind, and hold them there, jamming them if necessary.

Now the sails will balance each other and if the cat tries to move forward the rudders will steer it up towards the wind, which will kill the speed.

Try heaving-to in an area away from any obstacles or lee shores – it is very relaxing after zooming around!

RETURNING TO THE SHORE

You have had a good sail and are now on your way back to the beach. Choose a cross-wind landing so the boat arrives on a reach in an area clear of obstacles and other craft. A good distance from the beach – about 20 boat lengths – ask the crew to release the jib and raise the leeward centreboard (if fitted). At the same time release the mainsheet to slow the boat down, but not so much that it stops. If you are the helmsman, cross to the leeward side on your knees and lift the leeward rudder so it is just in the water. Then return to the windward side and slowly sail the boat towards the beach using the mainsail *only* as an accelerator and steering from the tiller connecting bar.

As you reach the beach, head the boat into the wind, lift the windward rudder and centreboard (if fitted) and ease out all the mainsheet and traveller line. The crew should slide into the water from the windward hull, in front of the shrouds, make his way to the bow and bridle wires and hold the boat head-to-wind. This way he cannot be run down by the boat if it accelerates again!

With the boat safe and sound, the crew should hold the bow and bridle wire while, as helmsman, you release the tension on the luff of the mainsail and detach the mainsheet.

You can drop the sails while on the water, or on the beach, but only if you keep the boat pointing into the wind.

Take down the jib first, because it will be damaged if you leave it flapping for too long. Release the jib downhaul line and unhook the halyard lock by alternately pulling the jib up with the halyard and down at the tack (bottom front corner). Then pull the sail down and roll it up from the head (top).

◆   To drop the jib, pull the peak up with the halyard while pulling down on the tack. This will release the hook and allow you to lower the sail.

To lower the mainsail on most modern catamarans, pull up on the main halyard to raise the halyard ring. While keeping the halyard tensioned turn the mast to *port*, which swings the mast hook away from the ring and frees the sail. Finally release the tension on the halyard and lower the sail. There are various other forms of masthead and jib halyard locks, but the basic principles are the same. Make sure you de-tension the battens before rolling the sail and stowing it away. Never leave the sails up if you intend to leave your boat unattended.

◆ To drop the main, remove the sail from the groove and pull the halyard. ◆   Rotate the mast to port to swing the masthead hook away from the locking ring at the peak of the sail. ◆   Release the halyard and pull down on the tack to lower the sail.

PART TWO:

SKILL DEVELOPMENT

Reaching

Remember: reaching is sailing *across* the wind. It is the fastest point of sailing but the jib, mainsail, trim and balance need constant adjustment for maximum speed.

MEDIUM WINDS

Trim
Constantly move the crew weight fore-and-aft to keep the (painted) waterline at the bow just covered – as the wind increases you will need to move slightly aft, but as the wind drops the stern will dig in and you will need to slide forward again. If you are too far forward you will get steering problems, while if you are too far back you will lose boatspeed.

Balance
Most catamarans like to be sailed with the windward hull just clear of the water on a reach, so move your crew weight inboard (and forward)

● **Reaching in medium winds: both helm and crew are sitting on the windward hull, the traveller is halfway down and the set of the sail is being controlled with the mainsheet.**

or outboard (and back) to balance the wind. Never heel the boat to windward.

Setting the sails
Set the jib so that the telltails on each side of the sail are flowing constantly. Position the traveller so that when the mainsheet is pulled in the top set of telltales are flowing and there is a *slight* twist in the leech (back edge) of the mainsail. The exact position of the traveller will depend on the type of reach (close or broad) and the speed at which the boat is travelling, but make sure that if the boat accelerates and the apparent wind moves forward, you can sheet in the mainsail to reset the telltales without pulling the traveller inboard. Experimenting with the traveller position, mainsheet position and vang (kicking strap) tension will help you create a smooth airflow across the entire area of the sail.

Going faster
Concentrate on keeping the sails set to the apparent wind, which changes with each alteration in the boatspeed. Try to use your rudders as little as possible, so that they don't act as brakes, and steer round any large waves that might stop the boat. On the racecourse, steer straight to the next mark (if the other competitors will let you).

Set the centreboards half up, if you have them. On a close reach push them down a little further and on a broad reach pull them up a little. If you feel the boat is tripping over itself it is often a good idea to raise the windward board a bit. (All these centreboard pointers apply to any windstrength on a reach).

LIGHT WINDS

Trim
The crew must sit forward, his head to windward of the mast, and watch the jib constantly. The wind is always changing in speed and direction but at slow speeds the boat takes a long time to alter course, so rather than have the helmsman saw away at the tiller it is better to adjust the sheets to each change.

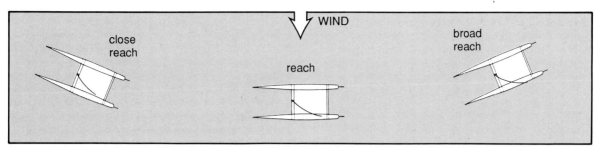

Balance
Generally keep the boat level, but in some instances it may well pay to have the leeward hull slightly deeper in the water.

Setting the sails
Tension the mainsail battens to produce maximum fullness a third of the way back, and tension the jib halyard to give maximum fullness of jib (slacker than for strong or medium winds). The tension on the mainsail downhaul need not be excessive, but has to be tight enough to remove the creases from the batten pockets.

When sailing on a reach in light winds allow the sails as much fullness as possible, and never over-sheet (pull the sheets too tight). Pulling in the mainsheet so the top of the mainsail leech is hooked is the most common mistake.

◆ Reaching in light winds: the helm and crew are well forward and inboard. The sheets need constant adjustment in these conditions.

Going faster
As with medium winds use as little rudder as possible, though you may want to bear off in a gust. Make all your body movements smooth and your sail alterations gentle. If your jib and mainsheet blocks have ratchets fitted, switch them off to allow the sheets to run easily.

STRONG WINDS

In strong winds there is considerable power in the sails on a reach and the forward pressure will constantly force the leeward bow down.

Trim
The helmsman should be as far back as possible. So should the crew: one foot will be aft of the

◆ Reaching in strong winds: the crew is on the trapeze to keep the boat level, and both helm and crew are well back to counteract any tendency to nosedive.

rear beam, and he will lower himself on the trapeze adjuster so he is horizontal. He will also be securely hooked to the restraining line.

If you are the helmsman, you will really have to work hard keeping the windward hull out of the water, avoiding nosedives and playing the waves. You will be sitting against the rear beam, sitting out hard and sheeting hard so that the leeward hull is just above the surface of the water. You will be sailing on a knife edge and must watch out for the approaching gust on the water, ready to ease the sheet as soon as it hits and avoid the sudden lifting of the hull which may cause you to dump the sheet, let the hull down hard and dunk the crew in the water.

Sail trim

Keep the sails set to the telltales as much as possible. If the boat is going to capsize, spill wind from the mainsail. If at any point the boat is hit by a gust and the acceleration causes the leeward bow to plough under, threatening a 'cartwheel', ease out the jib to reduce the pressure and if necessary reduce the power in the mainsail. You will notice that the tremendous acceleration and deceleration will change the apparent wind quite considerably so you need to make rapid sheet alterations.

Going faster

Concentrate on keeping the boat 'wound up' and going at full speed. Don't use too much rudder

◆ If a gust makes the leeward bow plough under, ease the jibsheet to reduce power and stop the boat cartwheeling.

but look out for waves that might stop the boat: luff a little as the bow hits a trough, climb the back of the next wave, then bear away on the crest. When a gust hits, ease the sails slightly and then pull them back in when the boat is up to speed. Make sure the crew has his weight out and back as far as possible.

CONTROLLING THE TILLER, MAINSHEET AND TRAVELLER

♠ Normally you hold the tiller over your shoulder and control the mainsheet with your other hand.

♠ To sheet in, haul on the mainsheet and clamp it against the tiller extension with your thumb.

♠ Then catch hold of the mainsheet below the point where you have clamped it, and haul away again.

♠ In a blow, use both hands to haul in the sheet while bracing the tiller against your shoulder.

♠ Clamp the sheet with your tiller hand while you reach down to grasp it nearer the block.

♠ Grab the sheet lower down with your tiller hand as well, and haul in again.

♠ To control the traveller, use your tiller hand to clamp the mainsheet while you pick up the line.

♠ Adjust the traveller to suit the sailing conditions, using your foot to cleat the line.

Beating

No boat can sail straight into the wind, that is from A to B in the diagram. If you try, the wind will simply pass either side of the sail and the boat will be blown backwards. The only way to get from A to B is to sail a zig-zag course at an angle of about 45° to the wind.

To do this you need the sails pulled right in, both the jib and mainsail. The crew will need to balance the boat by leaning out hard, probably on the trapeze. The course sailed is a compromise between boatspeed and the shortest distance to your goal. If you point too close to the wind the boat will slow down, but you will get closer to your goal. If you point away from the wind you will go faster but sail further away from your goal and travel further.

The simple way to check how close to the wind you can sail is to watch the front of your jib. With the sails pulled in, turn towards the wind until the front of the sail begins to flap, then turn back, away from the wind, until the flapping *just* stops. You are now sailing as close to the wind as possible without losing speed. Repeat this manoeuvre every few seconds to check your course.

If you are sailing without a jib you will have to sail more by the feel of the boat, because the mainsail is fully battened and will not flap. Turn towards the wind until the boat starts to lose speed and becomes sluggish. Turn away from the wind to let it pick up speed and become responsive.

When travelling from A to B you will need to tack at X and Y. (The method of tacking is given in the next chapter). When you tack you will pass through the no-go zone before sailing off at approximately 90° to your original course.

MEDIUM WINDS

Setting the sails
When beating in average winds pull the mainsail and jib in tight. Put the jibsheet in the jammers at position 2 (see opposite), but keep the mainsheet free for any adjustment. The correct tension on the mainsheet is critical and it should be set so that the leech (back) of the mainsail has a slight twist to leeward.

In strong winds the twist will increase and you will need more tension on the mainsheet. In lighter winds less twist is generated so you will need less mainsheet tension to hold the leech straight.

The telltales provide a good indication that you have achieved the right sail balance. When the windward telltale on the jib stalls, the top windward telltale on the mainsail should stall too. This means both sails are stalling together, which is ideal.

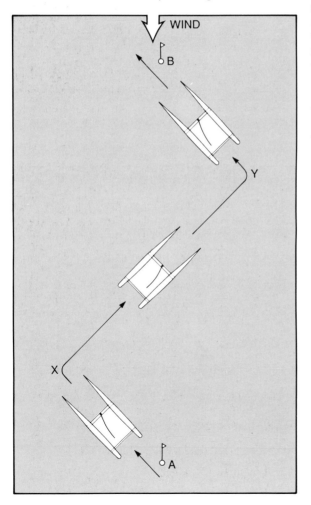

● If the main is sheeted too tight the leech hooks to windward.

● With too little sheet tension the leech is too open for efficiency.

● With no wind in the sail, the right tension gives a straight leech.

MARKING THE SHEETS

It is well worth marking the principal sheeting positions with a waterproof pen. To do this, find a sheltered part of the beach and turn the boat head-to-wind. Then:

1 Make sure the sheeting position of the blocks is equal on both sides of the boat relative to the main beam.

2 Sheet the jib hard on one side and mark the sheet with a waterproof pen where it passes through the camcleat on the block.

3 Measure the distance between the jib clew and the block.

4 Move the jib to the other side and cleat it so the distance is the same and make a mark at the new camcleat.

You now have the hardest tension you will need on each sheet. Ideally at this stage you should go sailing in a force 4 and test the positions.

5 Put the sheets back in the cams at the black marks and mark two further points at 10cm intervals on each sheet as you release them. Treat the marks as positions 3, 2 and 1 at the cam cleat.

Only one point on the mainsheet need be marked as a reference point (most catamarans require a 7:1 minimum purchase, so the amount of mainsheet hauled in or out when adjusting the sail is quite substantial).

On the beach, with the boat head-to-wind, tension the main luff downhaul, tension the mainsheet and walk back about three metres. Imagine a straight line between the head of the sail and the clew and then tension the mainsheet so that the ends of the battens lie along this line. Pull in a further 20cm and mark the sheet at this point.

Centreboard position

When beating, the wind creates the maximum amount of sideways force. To resist this make sure the centreboards (if fitted) are right down. Catamarans without centreboards should have as much of the leeward hull as possible immersed in the water. Keeping the windward hull just kissing the water gives maximum boatspeed in most wind conditions.

Trim

The position of your crew weight is important to performance when beating. Too far towards the back of the boat and the stern will drag in the water and the rudders will become heavy to use. Too far forward and the bows will try to keep going in a straight line whatever you do, and you will need to use a lot of rudder to change direction. With the crew weight in the correct position the stern is just out of the water with the bow cutting cleanly through the waves. If the boat has a waterline marked, keep it parallel to the water. Ideally, the helm and crew should be close together to let the ends of the hulls ride the waves easily.

On the beat, a catamaran sails most efficiently with one hull just kissing the water.

If the weight is too far forward it is hard to steer.

Too far back, and the transoms will drag in the water and slow you down.

Keep the waterline level for a clean passage through the water.

Course made good

No sailing boat is 100% efficient: when beating to windward the boat will always make a certain amount of sideways slip, or leeway. When planning your zig-zag route against the wind you must allow for this when passing obstructions, and also allow for any tide.

Gusts

Nothing about the wind is constant. Gusts can often be seen on the water as dark moving patches.

As a gust hits you the boat will accelerate under the increased power and you may need to lean out further. If the gust is strong enough to lift the windward hull out of the water, ease out the mainsheet to spill some wind out of the sail. Try to do this without altering course: pointing the boat towards the wind (luffing) will stall both sails and slow you down.

Windshifts

The wind changes in direction as well as strength. Some changes are small while others are quite dramatic, sometimes as much as 20°-30°, and can last much longer. Obviously you will need to adjust your course to take advantage of each windshift.

Lulls

If there are gusts there are also likely to be lulls. Make sure you re-balance and trim your boat, as it slows down, and if necessary ease out a few inches of mainsheet to take advantage of the conditions.

LIGHT WINDS

Trim

The crew should be well forward, curled around the mast with his elbow on the beam to windward. The helmsman should be on the weather deck in front of the shroud. The idea is to keep the waterline constantly covered; with a non-centreboard boat, the bow should be well dug in.

Sail trim

Use the top leeward telltale of the mainsail as a guide. It should stream across the back of the sail. If you overtension the mainsheet the sail will hook and the telltale will be all over the place.

◆ This may look exciting, but it is not the fastest way to sail! Keep the windward hull just clipping the wavetops.

◗ In light winds, get as far forward as you can to keep the waterline covered.

The leech of the jib must remain open (between positions 1 and 2) so that the flow of the wind between the leech of the jib and the luff of the mainsail is not throttled.

It is essential that as the windspeed increases both the mainsheet and jibsheet are tensioned, and as the puff eases the sheets are released. For the jibsheet you may be talking about only 2-3 cm and for the mainsheet 10-20cm.

As the helmsman, you will be fine-tuning the direction of the boat all the time, sailing with the luff of the jib just about to lift. You can afford to 'pinch' a bit in a puff, but you must keep the boat moving in the lulls.

Setting the sails
Be careful not to pull the jib in too tight, because this will destroy the sail shape and narrow the slot between the jib and mainsail. The mainsheet tension should be just sufficient to bring the leech almost in line with the centreline of the boat. Too much tension in the mainsheet or vang (kicker) will cause the leech to hook over to the windward side in light winds, a sure way of losing speed.

Going faster
Sail the boat free – do not 'pinch' too close to the wind. It is imperative that you keep the boat moving to give steerage and keep the air flowing over the sails.

STRONG WINDS

The method of sailing to windward in strong winds varies according to your all-up crew weight. Heavy crews can sail free and power along while lighter crews will need to luff up into the wind slightly, spilling wind and going slower – but pointing higher.

Trim
Arrange your weight to prevent the boat pitching; usually this means placing the crew just behind the shrouds.

Balance
Keep the boat almost flat, with the windward hull just kissing the water.

Setting the sails
Initially have both sails in tight. The stronger the wind the more the leech of the mainsail will try to fall away and the more mainsheet tension is needed to close it. The jib is pulled in to position 3. As you start to become overpowered, ease out the mainsheet to spill wind and keep the windward hull kissing the wavetops.

- If you get out on the wire and try to keep the boat level on the water it will go faster and be easier to sail.

- If you have centreboards, push them right down on the beat to minimise leeway.

BEATING PROBLEMS

Mistake	Effect
The sails are not sheeted in tight enough	The boat has no power
The traveller line is not pulled in	The boat will not sail close to the wind
The crew weight is too great or the boat is not level	The rudders feel 'heavy'
Pointing too close to the wind	The boat travels slowly and is sluggish to steer
Pointing too far off the wind	The boat is sailing fast through the water, but not making windward progress
There is too much wind in the sail	The windward hull is way out of the water – cure by easing mainsheet or pointing closer to the wind

In very strong winds the amount you can 'dump' the mainsheet is restricted by the air flowing through the slot off the jib, which stops the fully-battened mainsail from spilling wind. This can also make the mast bend in reverse and rotate to windward, which can break it.

The solution is to ease the jib slightly to open the slot, ease the traveller a little and sheet the mainsail in as tight as possible. This effectively means that the mainsail is driving the boat to windward with the jib luffing slightly.

Going faster
Continually reset the sails for maximum power. Watch out for waves and feed the boat over them, moving your weight to assist the boat's passage through the water. If you are too far forward the main beam will catch the waves, while if you are too far back the bow will slam and the transom will drag.

Centreboards
Keep the centreboards down at all times.

Tacking

Tacking a catamaran is not like tacking a dinghy, and it is a good idea to practise the sequence on land so you are familiar with the necessary movements.

Place the boat on a soft surface such as grass or sand, and connect the rudder assembly. With the sails down, clip the mainsheet to the main halyard.

As the helmsman, sit on one side of the boat with your feet under the toestraps, your front hand (nearest the bow) holding the mainsheet and your back hand holding the tiller in a dagger grip on your shoulder. Fix in your mind that you are beating against the wind, with the sails pinned in, and that you are going to tack. Check that the boat is 'sailing' as close to the wind as possible, the sails pulled in tight, traveller right in, centreboard down (if fitted). Give the order 'Ready to tack', check the sailing area, and move your feet so that your back leg is bent under your front leg outside the toestraps. Place the spare mainsheet in the centre of the trampoline and prepare to tack.

Initiate the turning of the boat by pushing the tiller away until the rudders are at 45° to the hulls. This should be done in a firm steady movement rather like sailing a cruiser or driving a big lorry, not too gently or too violently.

Wait until the mainsail and bows 'point into the wind', then start to move across the boat by rolling onto the knee of your back leg, and face towards the back of the boat. Pass the tiller around the back of the mainsheet falls. At this point you should be kneeling, facing backwards, rudders *still* at 45°. Change hands and move to the new hull. Centralise your rudders when the sails have settled on the new tack.

Crew jobs
Because the boat is sailing against the wind you will have to pull the jib in fully. When the helmsman calls 'Ready to tack' check the sailing area, call 'All clear' (if it is!) and prepare to cross the boat by tucking your front foot under your back leg. As the boat turns, un-jam the jib sheets and move to the centre of the boat facing forward on your knees. Keep an eye on the jib: you are waiting for the wind to push on the reverse side of the sail. At the point when the sail fills on the reverse side free the jib sheet and pull in on the new side from the jamming cleat; this will ensure the jib flaps as little as possible between tacks.

Tacking is an art and requires timing, fluency and teamwork! Now let's try it on the water.

TACKING IN MEDIUM WINDS

A medium-wind tack should be a simple, fast, efficient turn which leaves the boat with good speed when settled on the new windward course. Sheet the sails fully and initiate the turn by

▼ **Push the tiller away . . .**   ▼ **Kneel and start to move across . . .**   ▼ **Change hands . . .**

TACKING PROBLEMS

Mistake	Effect
Not tightening the mainsheet fully before the tack	The boat does not turn head-to-wind
Not sailing on the edge of no-go zone	The boat is slow in tacking
Sailing inside the no-go zone	The boat is sailing too slowly before the tack
Moving too quickly across the boat	The boat is slow in tacking
Not holding the rudder at 45° throughout the tack	The boat loses speed in the turn
The traveller is slack	The boat is slow to reach head-to-wind
Allowing the mainsheet to run out as you tack	The boat loses speed in the turn
Letting go the jib too early, so that it flaps	Loss of speed
Keeping the jib aback too long	The boat is slow to accelerate on the new tack

turning the rudders to 45° before crossing the boat. Move your legs as described for tacking practice on land, so your body crosses the boat smoothly.

It is helpful to release the mainsheet by a few inches in the middle of the tack to help the battens flick over. When you sheet the mainsail back in, the boat will accelerate away on its new course.

TACKING IN LIGHT WINDS

When tacking in light winds you must move smoothly to keep the boat going and to encourage air to flow over the sails for as long as possible.

1   Apply smooth but firm pressure on the helm and don't straighten up until the tack is complete. Keep the mainsheet tension fairly light as you enter the tack to prevent the leech hooking. To help spin the boat, pull in the mainsheet as the boat turns towards head-to-wind.

2   Move to the rear of the boat and pass the tiller extension behind the mainsheet, taking care not to jerk the tiller. It is important to release the sheet immediately the boat passes through the eye of the wind. Let out approximately 60cm of sheet and quickly flick the clew to ensure the battens pop across in one movement.

3   As the new course is taken up, tension the mainsheet as the boat accelerates – no sudden jerks – and quickly adjust it so the wind flows around the back of the sail.

↟ Swivel the tiller extension over . . .   ↟ Settle down on the other side . . .   ↟ . . . and straighten up.

♠ **Get some speed** . . .   **Come head-to-wind** . . .   **Move across the boat** . . .

4 Move your weight forward as quickly as possible.

Crew
1 Release the sheet from the cam on the order 'Ready about' – but keep your weight forward near the mainbeam.
2 Ensure that the sheet is fully clear for passing through the block.
3 On 'Lee-o', do not release the sheet but watch the wind indicator carefully. Just before head-to-wind release the old sheet and gently start sheeting in the new one, watching the wind indicator at all times. If you have to, back the sail by holding it on the 'old' side so it fills on the wrong side. This will push the bows round.
4 Move your weight forward, and check the mast has rotated.
5 Tension the jibsheet to its mark position as the boat accelerates.

♦ **Be sure not to apply too much rudder when you start the turn, or you may stop the boat dead in the water.**

Change hands . . .   Settle on the new side . . .   . . . and sail away.

TACKING IN STRONG WINDS

Strong-wind tacking also demands good timing and boatspeed. You may have eased the mainsail to prevent capsizing when sailing to windward; this will cause drag if the sail is allowed to flag as the boat moves through the tack, so remember to sheet in first. Waves will also stop the bows turning.

Helmsman
1 Look ahead for a flat patch.
2 Shout 'Ready about'. When the crew is on the trampoline start to turn. *Do not* release the mainsheet if the windward hull lifts – the tension in the leach is needed to push the stern around. Pull in the mainsheet hard as the bows approach head-to-wind – the last 60cm are vital.
3 Move quickly to the centre of the boat, maintaining pressure on the helm, and pass the extension onto the other side just in front of the rear beam. Your forward hand is holding the fall of the sheet – pass this hand around the traveller and grab the tiller extension, making sure the turning pressure is kept on.
4 Just after the boat passes through the wind the battens will 'pop' across, and by that time you should be nearly across the boat, with the sheet in your forward hand. On hearing the 'pop' immediately release a metre of sheet.
5 Straighten up. As soon as the crew is on the wire on the new side, pull in the mainsheet and move forward.

Crew
1 On the command 'Ready about' uncleat the jibsheet and check the rope is ready to run.
2 On 'Lee-o' come onto the trampoline and cross the boat just aft of the shrouds. As you get better you should delay coming off the trapeze for as long as possible.
3 Watch the wind indicator and 'feel' the boat's progress. Ideally you should release the jib before it backs, but you may need to back it if the turn is too slow.
4 When about 20° onto the new tack, release the old sheet and, as quickly as possible, pull in the new sheet. Hook on to the trapeze and go out. The boat cannot gain speed until you have completed the tack.

STOPPING HEAD-TO-WIND

If you get stopped you will have to do a 'three-point turn'. You will only get stopped if:
● A wave has hit the boat – the helmsman chose a bad place to tack.
● The rudders have been released half-way through the tack.
● Maximum tension was not kept on the mainsheet.

● The crew released the jibsheet too soon.
   You will now be going backwards. To get
going:
1   Hold the jib aback.
2   Put the rudders hard over to the other side.
3   Release a lot of mainsheet.
4   When you have swung round onto the course
for the new tack, release the jibsheet and sheet in
on the new side.
5   Only now can you pull in the mainsheet and
accelerate away on the new tack.

**1.   The boat goes into the tack too
slowly to complete it.**

**2.   The boat stops and the wind starts
to blow it backwards.**

**3.   Release the mainsheet and reverse
the rudder to bring the boat onto the
new tack.**

**4.   With the boat pointing the right
way, straighten the rudders and haul
in the mainsheet to get going.**

5.   Sailing again!

Running

All catamarans can run with the wind directly behind them, but because of their incredible speed in relation to the wind's strength it is generally far more efficient to 'tack' downwind in a zig-zag fashion (rather like beating against the wind).

You will soon find that there is an optimum angle for sailing downwind, just as there is for sailing upwind. This angle is normally 90° to the *apparent wind*.

Apparent wind
The word *apparent* is a good way of describing the direction of the wind given on your wind indicator or flag when the boat is travelling at speed. When a boat is at rest the direction of the wind indicator is a true indication of the real direction of the wind, but as the boat accelerates it creates a second wind blowing from the front. This second wind and the real wind combine to become the *apparent wind*. This can be likened to putting your hand out of a car window when the car is moving: although the true wind may be blowing across the car it will feel as though the wind is blowing from the front because the car is travelling forward through the air.

Apparent wind enables a catamaran to 'tack' downwind at speed and should be kept at 90° to the boat.

MEDIUM WINDS

In medium winds you will need to ease the traveller right out and ease the mainsheet until the sail just touches the shrouds – any further than this and the sail will deform around the shrouds and its aerodynamic properties will be lost. Set the traveller right out to reduce the twist in the leech (back edge) of the sail and ease the jibsheet until the luff (front) of the jib is about to flap. Now your sails are set for downwind sailing.

Centreboard position
When sailing downwind the centreboards, if fitted, can usually be retracted completely. The depth of the hull in the water is normally sufficient to give control. In adverse conditions or to give more 'feel' on the rudders you may need to expose a small amount of centreboard.

Balance
Crew weight will need to be distributed evenly between the two hulls. In moderate conditions this often means that the helm and crew are on opposite sides of the boat, with the crew holding the clew of the jib to keep it well away from the mainsail. The jib telltales are good indicators of the best position. As the wind increases the crew may need to move towards the centre or

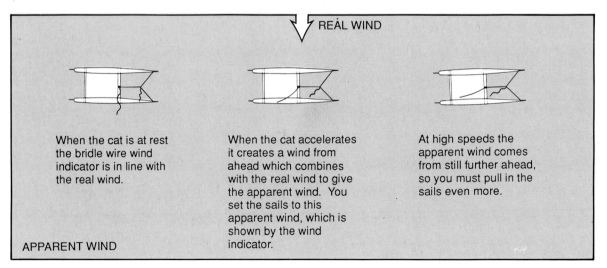

REAL WIND

When the cat is at rest the bridle wire wind indicator is in line with the real wind.

When the cat accelerates it creates a wind from ahead which combines with the real wind to give the apparent wind. You set the sails to this apparent wind, which is shown by the wind indicator.

At high speeds the apparent wind comes from still further ahead, so you must pull in the sails even more.

APPARENT WIND

windward side of the boat to keep both hulls in balance.

Trim

Downwind the fore-and-aft trim is very sensitive. Normally you should try to keep the boat level and the transom just out of the water. In lighter winds move further forward, while in strong winds you should both move back dramatically to stop the bows digging in.

Course made good

The shortest distance between points A and B in the diagram is a straight line downwind, but for catamarans this is not the quickest way.

Instead you should keep the bridle-wire wind indicator at 90° to the boat, giving you a zig-zag course to point B, gybing occasionally.

The stronger the wind the faster the boat will go, and the stronger the apparent wind becomes relative to the real wind, the broader the angle you can sail downwind.

You should also use the top, leeward telltale on the mainsail. The aim is to get maximum leeway without stalling out the sails – that is, letting the telltale drop. As soon as it does drop, the flow of wind over the back of the sail will have broken down and the only way of recovering it is to head up, making the boat accelerate. As the speed builds, the apparent wind will come forward, flow will build up over the mainsail again and you can slowly bear away – but not too far or the sail will stall and the whole process has to be started again.

Downwind sailing does therefore involve quite substantial changes in direction, particularly for the inexperienced as they repeatedly stall out and have to accelerate. As experience and feel increase, the deviations become less and less until the vital knife-edge is found where the mainsail never stalls out.

The crew plays a major role, working with the helm to keep all the telltales parallel and quickly adjusting to any change in direction of the boat or the wind. It is vitally important to hook on to the new wind direction over the sail, and as the helm bears away, ease the jibsheet gently with the change of direction.

● When you are sailing fast in a blow the apparent wind moves forward, so you can aim more directly for your goal while still keeping the wind indicator at 90° to the boat.

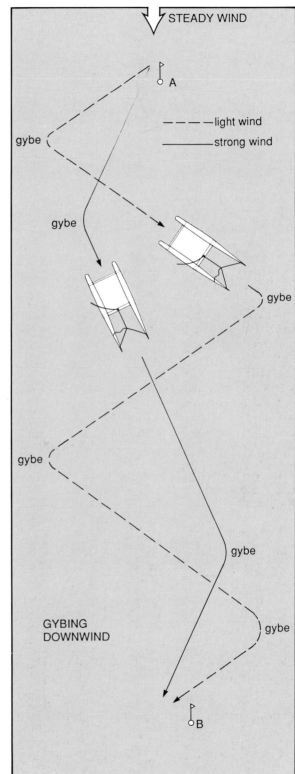

STEADY WIND

A

——————— light wind
——————— strong wind

gybe

gybe

gybe

gybe

gybe

gybe

gybe

GYBING DOWNWIND

B

REAL WIND

here the boat is going
too slowly, with the
indicator forward

luff to pick
up speed

as the boat accelerates
the indicator begins
to stream back

bear away gently,
keeping up speed

as the speed drops
the indicator will
blow forward again

luff to pick up
speed again

STEERING A COURSE DOWNWIND

The helmsman may well ask 'what direction am I going to go in when I gybe?' If he is on a true downwind course with the apparent wind at right angles, the crew can look straight down the beams to give him the heading of the next course.

Gusts

When a gust hits the sails the boat will immediately accelerate, initially causing the bows to bury. React by moving your weight back and by keeping both hulls in the water.

Also if you look at the bridle wire wind indicator it will be blowing towards the stern rather than at 90°, because the apparent wind has increased. Turn away from the wind to bring the indicator back to 90°.

If at any point the gusts become severe and the bow really buries, react by releasing the jibsheet.

Lulls

When the wind gets lighter the boat will slow down and the apparent wind will decrease in strength. This will allow the true wind direction to take over and the bridle wire wind indicator will blow forward of 90°.

If you do not react by turning the boat up towards the wind to get the indicator blowing at 90° to the boat again the sails will stall and the boat will slow down even more.

Windshifts

If, when sailing downwind, a windshift forces you to steer further away from your goal, then gybe. If the windshift takes you nearer to your goal use it to your advantage, but do not sail too far before gybing to reach your destination.

Summing up

Sailing downwind in catamarans is basically a series of broad reaches keeping the wind indicator at 90° to the boat. Because the wind varies slightly in strength and apparent direction the course sailed will not be straight, but a meandering line which is always at 90° to the direction of the apparent wind.

Since a cat sails most efficiently with the wind indicator at 90° to the boat, you should always steer to keep it at that angle. You will find that as you accelerate you can bear away, but if you lose speed you will have to luff up again.

♠ Running in medium winds. Note that the traveller is as far across as it will go, allowing the helmsman to control the shape of the sail with the mainsheet.

♠ If there are windshifts, gybe on them to steer a more direct course to your goal. You may gybe more frequently than you would in a steady wind, but it's worth it.

LIGHT WINDS

As always in light winds, move as gently as possible to avoid shaking the shape out of the sails.

Trim
Sit forward of the balance point to bring the transom out of the water and depress the bows slightly. The crew should be on the leeward main beam.

Balance
To balance the boat the crew and helmsman should be on either side of the boat, one on each hull.

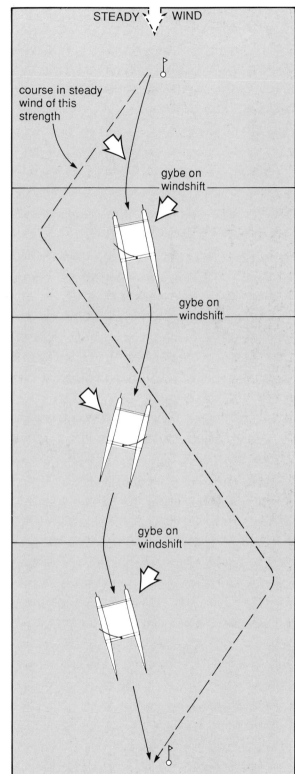

STEADY WIND

course in steady wind of this strength

gybe on windshift

gybe on windshift

gybe on windshift

● In light winds, keep the boat level by sitting one on either hull, and well forward to stop the transoms dragging in the water.

Setting the sails

Allow the sails to be as far forward as possible. The crew can manually hold out the jib with his free hand and keep the mast in its fully rotated position with his foot.

Going faster

In light winds it is very easy to stall the sails. Try pointing higher into the wind than usual to get the boat moving before bearing away downwind. In the very lightest winds it sometimes pays to sail *almost* dead downwind.

STRONG WINDS

This is where the excitement starts . . .

Trim

Sit back to keep the boat level, fore-and-aft. At these speeds if the bows dip under the water the boat may cartwheel or pitchpole unless the crew reacts immediately by moving further back.

Balance

By holding the boat on an even keel, the downward pressure on the bow is shared

DOWNWIND PROBLEMS

Mistake	Effect
The mainsail is in too tight	The sail stalls
The jib is in too tight	Air cannot flow over the back of the mainsail
The traveller is on the centreline of the boat	This puts too much twist in the mainsail and makes it less efficient
The mainsail is out too far	The battens are distorted round the shroud
The jib is out too far	Too little air is being forced round the back of the mainsail and both sails flap
The crew weight is too far back	The bow is in the air and the transom is dragging
The crew weight is all on one side	The boat is out of balance
The bridle wire wind indicator is forward of 90°	The sails are stalled and the boat loses speed
The wind indicator is aft of 90°	The boat is not heading as far downwind as it could
The bow buries	The crew weight is too far forward or the sails are wrongly set

between both hulls. Generally the crew will be on the windward deck by the shroud.

Sail trim

Some mainsheet tension is needed to stop the sail distorting around the shroud.

Because the crew is on the windward side, the jib is controlled through the jibsheet block. If, owing to gusts or waves, the bow begins to bury you should immediately free the jib to reduce the pressure on the bow. As soon as the bow has popped back up, pull the jib in the keep up the boatspeed. Often it is only the initial strength of the gust that forces the bow down. Sometimes in extreme conditions even this is not enough and you will have to head the boat away downwind to stall the sails slightly.

When conditions are extreme and the boat is continually tripping over itself, de-power the mainsail by sheeting it in and pulling in the traveller a little. This will spoil the airflow somewhat and decrease the pressure on the bows.

Cartwheeling

When the bow of one hull is forced down, either by the drive in the sails or by a wave stopping the boat, you may find yourself cartwheeling. The effect is to pivot the boat up and over on the point of the bow, throwing the helm and crew

♠ **If you dig the bows in on a run (left) the leeward hull is likely to plough under (centre), the stern will flip up and the boat will start to cartwheel (right).**

forward into the sail or water. The experience can be quite exhilarating!

To prevent this happening, get the crew to keep an eye on the bow; when he sees it starting to bury he can release the jibsheet to reduce the pressure on the bow. On a reach the helmsman can help by easing out the mainsail. Do *not* bear away or luff up as this will only aggravate the situation. Cartwheeling is often also caused by bearing away without easing out the sheets, which causes tremendous pressure on the leeward bow.

Pitchpoling

Pitchpoling occurs when both hulls are forced under the water at the same time, causing the boat to stop very abruptly and lifting the stern end right out of the water, and over. This normally happens only on windy days with severe gusts, when the boat trips over itself going downwind (a cat rarely pitchpoles on a reach and never on a beat).

To prevent pitchpoling, keep the boat level on the water for more bow buoyancy, turn the boat further downwind and pull in the mainsail to depower the rig. If she starts to go down, release the jib.

Gybing

The best thing about gybing is that, unlike tacking, you can guarantee it will take place! However, gybing a catamaran requires a large amount of sea room and full boat control. Practise first on the beach without sails before trying it on the water.

Helmsman

1 Steer the boat onto a downwind course with the bridle wire wind indicator at 90° across the boat. The sails should be set as far out as possible, the jib so it is not quite flapping, the mainsail almost touching the shroud and the traveller right out. The centreboards (if fitted) should be up.

2 Prepare to gybe by tucking your back leg under the front as for tacking.

3 Initiate the turn by pulling the tiller towards you and move *immediately* across the boat on your knees, facing backwards, to the other hull.

4 Keeping the turn on, move the tiller over to the new side behind the mainsheet, change hands and put your *new* front hand on the falls of the mainsheet.

5 Wait for the sail to cross, centralise the rudders and check the movement of the falls before letting them cross to the other side.

6 Sit down looking forward and bring the boat back onto a downwind course with the bridle wire wind indicator at 90° across the boat.

Crew

1 Set the jib correctly and wait for the order to gybe.

2 When the helm gives the command 'Stand by to gybe', check the sailing area and, if all is well, answer 'All clear'. Tuck your front leg in under your back leg and tidy away the jibsheets forward of your body.

3 As the boat turns further downwind move to the middle of the boat and watch for the jib to collapse.

4 As this happens the mainsail will cross the boat and you can set the jib on the new side.

5 Reposition yourself to balance the boat and trim the hulls fore-and-aft.

GYBING IN LIGHT WINDS

As for tacking, the secret of gybing in light airs is smoothness of movement by both helmsman and crew. Keep your weight right forward and settle onto the new course quickly.

Helmsman

1 Warn the crew.

2 Begin the turn and move to the rear beam, passing the extension to the new windward transom.

➧ **To gybe the boat . . .**   ➧ **Pull the tiller towards you . . .**   ➧ **Swivel the extension across and grasp the mainsheet falls . . .**

GYBING PROBLEMS

Mistake	Effect
The sails are too far in (or out)	Too far in and you lose speed; too far out and the gybe is too violent
The boat is heading too far downwind (stalled) just before the gybe	You lose speed
The boat is not balanced or trimmed correctly	You risk a nosedive
The gybe was not initiated before crossing the boat	You lose control of the boat
Straightening the rudders too early	You lose the turn as you move from one side to the other
Not changing hands before the mainsail crosses	The mainsheet falls hit you
Not 'checking' the mainsheet falls as they cross	The boat screws up into the wind
Not looking forward after completing the gybe to bring the boat back onto a downwind course	The boat sails off in the wrong direction
Not straightening the rudders immediately after the mainsail crosses	The boat screws up into the wind

3 Let the wind do the work in passing the mainsail across. Take the falls of the mainsheet just below the clew, follow the sail across and, after it passes the centre, flick the mainsheet falls down and back to 'pop' the battens onto the new gybe.

4 Quickly return to the front of the boat and 'hook on' to the new wind.

Crew
You should be sitting on the lee deck on the main beam holding the sheet approximately one metre from the clew.

1 Move smoothly across the boat to a similar position on the other side.

2 Quickly get the telltales flowing parallel over the sail on the new side.

☛ **Check the falls as the sail crosses the boat . . .**

☛ **With the sail on the new side, straighten the rudders . . .**

☛ **Release the mainsheet and return to downwind sailing.**

◆ Start the turn . . .   Cross the tiller extension . . .   Hold the falls of the mainsheet . . .

Help the sail across . . .   Check the falls . . .   Settle down and sail off.

GYBING IN STRONG WINDS

The aim should be to gybe at maximum speed (and never when accelerating), and with the rudders deep in the water.

In really hard weather, the crew will be in the centre of the boat level with the shrouds with the helmsman just behind him.

Helmsman
1 Move to the back of the boat and prepare to gybe.
2 Initiate the turn by gently pulling the tiller extension towards you (since you are going fast you need less rudder movement to turn).

◆ **Get some speed before you gybe, then try to gybe in a lull while the boat is still travelling fast. This reduces the apparent wind and makes the manoeuvre less violent.**

3 Move across the boat on your knees and change hands as already described.
4 As the mainsail becomes ineffective pull the mainsheet falls to the centreline of the boat and check their movement as they cross to the other side (the boat should be pointing downwind at this stage).
5 As you check the mainsheet falls, centralise the rudders. In extreme conditions compensate for the kick of the mainsheet by pulling the tiller extension slightly to windward.
6 Once you have completed the gybe look forward, recover the mainsheet and return to downwind sailing using the downwind telltales.

Crew
The crew does not have a great influence on gybing. You should aim to keep your weight central and ensure the jib is quickly filled on the new gybe.

Trapezing

Trapezing is a method of extending your body weight out further from the side of the boat to give more righting effect. This allows you to harness more wind without the likelihood of capsizing, and hence increase your boatspeed. What's more, out on the trapeze the feeling of power and speed is tremendous!

The harness
The harness is rather like a nappy with a back support. It needs to be strapped firmly around your hips and adjusted at the shoulder straps so that your back is fully supported when in the trapezing position.

There are various styles of harness and each to his own, so try various types before you buy.

The trapeze wires
The trapeze wires are attached high up the mast and run down either side of the shrouds to a shock-cord restraining line. At the bottom end of each wire is a 'trapeze ring' and an adjustable line. The hook of your harness connects to the trapeze ring and the trapezing height is altered by the trapeze adjusting line.

HOW TO GET OUT THERE

It is a good idea to practise trapezing techniques on the beach before trying them afloat. Position the boat on some soft ground with the bows slightly raised.

◆   A strong, comfortable trapeze harness is essential equipment for the crew.

◆   The trapeze itself: the wire, handle, height adjustment block and ring, which is linked to the ring on the other side of the boat by a length of shockcord.

◆   The trapeze in action on a Tornado.

1 Settle into a normal beating position with the jib sheet in your back hand and your feet under the toestraps, and lean out over the side.

2 Place your front hand on the trapeze handle and transfer the jib sheets to it, attach your harness hook to the trapeze ring and transfer your weight on to the wire. Use your back hand for balance; if there is a toe loop nearby use it to prevent yourself from falling forward.

3 Twist your body towards the back of the boat and put your front leg up onto the side of the gunwhale (the edge of the deck). Push out and back to straighten your front leg and at the same time bend your back leg and position it on the side of the deck.

4 Fully extend your body, letting go with your hands and straightening your legs, front leg first.

Once you have settled into the trapezing position check your trapezing height: you should be level with the decks. If you are too high or too low alter your height by using the adjuster line. When you feel comfortable, relaxed and in the right position return the jibsheets to your back hand and put your front hand behind your head for extra leverage.

If you feel you are falling towards the bow, bend your back leg slightly. Your confidence will soon grow and you will then start to feel the movement of the boat through your feet. The toe loops are there to secure your position in rough seas but usually you will not use them because you will want to move your weight fore-and-aft to help trim the hull.

Trapezing height
The height at which you trapeze is subject to the conditions. Ideally you should trapeze level with the deck but in rough seas or light winds it is usually a good idea to be higher up.

Moonwalking
During the learning period you will inevitably lose your balance and swing forward. Once your back foot has lost contact with the hull and you have

● Grab the trapeze handle and sheet . . .

● Position your front leg and swing out . . .

● Extend your front leg and position your back leg . . .

● Straighten your legs and stretch right out.

pivoted forward on your front foot you have lost control and will end up against the side of the boat suspended from your trapeze wire.

A better alternative is to 'moon walk' forwards, returning to your original position when under control. So as soon as you feel you are going to swing forward and the bending of your back leg will not stop you, bounce down the edge of the gunwhale on the balls of your feet. When you've regained your balance you can work your way back to your original position, rather like a rock climber absailing down a mountain.

THE RESTRAINING LINE

Sometimes the boat is going so fast on a reach that the power of the sails forces the bows under the water. Retrim the boat by moving aft: for the crew (on the trapeze) this means walking back down the boat to a position behind the helmsman. Once there, the forward pull of the trapeze wire is tremendous, so most boats are fitted with a restraining line or 'hook back' which stops you sliding forward inadvertently.

How to get onto the restraining line
Starting off from the normal crewing trapeze position, take the jib sheet in your front hand, bend down and pick up the rstraining line in your back hand. Use the line to pull yourself back behind the helmsman and then clip it onto the trapeze ring. Now you are secure, but because you are further from the mast you are also trapezing higher off the water. Adjust the trapeze line until you are back level with the hull.

It is important that the helmsman now holds the tiller extension further towards the stern, or the end is likely to catch in your harness (or do something much worse!). You will have to hold the jibsheet in your forward hand to avoid the helmsman's head.

At the end of the reach prepare to move forward. Raise your position on the trapeze height adjuster and then unhook from the restraining line using your back hand. Don't let go, or you will fall forward: Hold onto the restraining line and walk forward. You can then let go of the line and trapeze normally.

● If the boat is still trying to heel, get your weight as far outboard as possible. Every little bit helps.

● When trapezing downwind, hook onto the restraining line and get to the back of the boat, behind the helmsman.

RETURNING TO THE BOAT

If the wind drops or you need to tack you will have to come back into the boat. To do this, first jam the jibsheet and transfer it to your forward hand which should also be holding the trapeze handle.

Take your feet out of the toe-loops and, bending your back leg more than your front one, swing back in over the edge. It is a good idea to lift your backside over the lip of the gunwhale by using your front hand on the handle.

Once back on board unhook the trapeze wire from your harness and return the jibsheet to your back hand ready for action.

TRAPEZING SINGLE-HANDED

The principles of single-handed trapezing are much the same, but it is important that the boat is set up right before you swing out –adjustments are not easy when you're out on the wire!

Fix the traveller position, transfer the mainsheet to your tiller hand and, using your front hand, hook onto the trapeze wire. Swing out

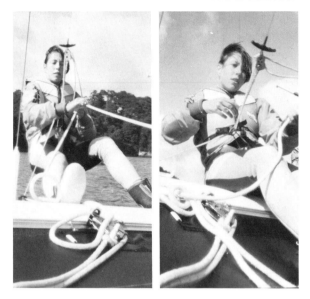

♠ To get back in, jam the jib sheet and bend your back leg (left) before swinging back into the boat (right).

♦ There is no rule that says the crew has to do the trapezing. If your crew is inexperienced, and as helm you feel capable of going out on the wire, then try it!

♦ Trapezing single-handed can be an exhilarating experience, but be careful not to lose your balance.

TRAPEZING PROBLEMS

Mistake	Effect
Not putting your weight on the wire after hooking on	The trapeze hook can unclip
Not relying on the hook, or unhooking when trapezing	All your weight is supported on your arm
Not keeping your front leg straight as you move out or as you are trapezing	You lose your balance and fall forward – counter this by always leading with your front foot, bending your back leg and using your back hand for balance
Trapezing too high on the wire	You feel as though you will fall back into the boat
Trapezing too low	You get knocked off by waves
Trapezing too far forward	The bows bury at speed – counter this by moving back onto the restraining line

over the side using your front hand on the trapeze handle for balance. Once out and fully extended transfer the mainsheet to your forward hand. You will find the boat very sensitive to your weight, fore and aft, and by using your legs the mainsheet is surprisingly easy to pull in. Loose sheets should be left on the trampoline and 'run' between your legs to stop them dragging in the water. Any violent rudder movement will make it difficult for you to keep your balance, so make sure you keep the rudders straight as you go out on the trapeze or come back in.

Man overboard!

Once you are reasonably confident about tacking, gybing and the three points of sailing, you will want to really turn on the speed.

This is when you are most likely to lose your crew over the side – maybe during an over-enthusiastic gybe, or by the crew losing his footing, or being caught unawares by a wave. Whatever the reason, it is essential that you can sail back without delay and pick up the unfortunate victim.

It is best to practise this in moderate winds – but remember you are much more likely to lose someone when conditions are not quite so pleasant.

1 As soon as the crew falls off the boat note his position, then release the jib so you have only the mainsail to contend with.

2 Sail off on a reach, keeping an eye on the man overboard.

3 When you consider you are far enough away, turn the boat downwind and gybe back towards him.

4 After the gybe pull the traveller almost right in and return to the victim on a close reach using the mainsheet as an accelerator. Jog the boat back towards the crew, being sure to allow for leeway.

● If you lose your crew over the side, release the jib so you can control the boat single-handed.

5 On reaching the crew use the last of the boatspeed to point into wind so the crew ends up alongside the windward hull, by the shroud.

6 Release the traveller and mainsheet; hold the rudders over (so the boat continues to point into the wind) and help the crew back aboard.

● Crew overboard!   ● Release the jib and sail off on a reach . .   ● Gybe round . . .

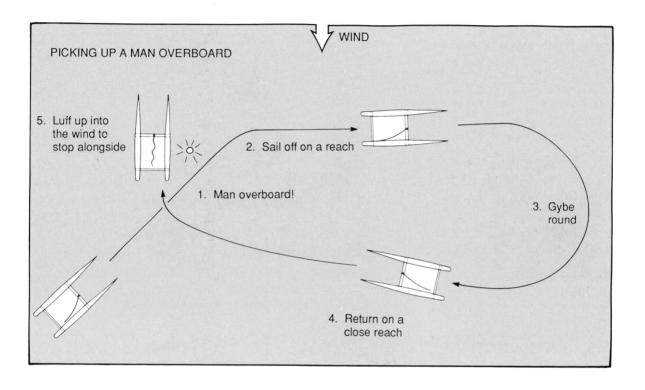

PICKING UP A MAN OVERBOARD

WIND

5. Luff up into the wind to stop alongside

2. Sail off on a reach

1. Man overboard!

3. Gybe round

4. Return on a close reach

Return on a close reach . . .

Turn into the wind alongside the crew . . .

And pull her aboard.

When approaching the victim in extreme conditions it is often better to stop the catamaran with the crew *between* the hulls by the main beam. This secures his position and allows you to retrieve him over the rear beam as in a capsize. It also prevents the bow, which has a large windage area, blowing away from the victim as you drift towards him.

◆ Steer carefully and stop with the crew between the hulls . . .

◆ The crew can then move under the trampoline to the back of the boat . . .

◆ . . . and, with a little help, haul herself back on board.

MAN OVERBOARD PROBLEMS

Mistake	Effect
Not releasing the jib	The boat is too powerful to manage easily singlehanded
Tacking instead of gybing	In strong winds, with the jib flapping you are unlikely to achieve a successful tack.
Not going far enough away to gybe	You cannot return to the victim on a close reach
Not coming back to the crew on a close reach	You arrive too fast, or out of position so you cannot pick up the crew to windward
Insufficient boatspeed on the final approach to the crew	You lose steerage at the critical moment

Capsize

All small catamarans are liable to capsize, and unless you want a sophisticated machine and have a great deal of experience the catamaran you choose must be easily righted after a capsize.

There are two possibilities: either the boat will lie on its side (90° capsize) or it will invert (180° capsize). Most modern catamarans have positive mast buoyancy to make them lie on their sides in the water, but a full inversion is always a possibility.

90° CAPSIZE AND RECOVERY

1   Since catamarans float high on their sides with a tremendous amount of windage, it is important that you keep in contact with the boat as it capsizes by holding on to the mainsheet or jibsheet, or it may blow away from you. The boat is your liferaft, so hang on!

2   Lower yourself into the water, preferably between the foot of the mainsail and the trampoline. Make sure you do not try to hold yourself out of the water, or you may pull the boat over on top of you.

3   Keep in contact with the boat, swim towards the bow and slide on to the lower hull, forward of the main beam.

4   Gently submerge the bow. This will bring the boat around until the mast is pointing into the wind, acting as a sea anchor.

5   Prepare the boat for righting by releasing the mainsheet, jibsheet and traveller. This is important, since otherwise the boat will sail away once it has been righted.

6   Position yourselves (both helm and crew) by the main beam and throw the righting line or the end of the mainsail halyard over the top hull. The amount of crew weight required to right the boat will depend on the type and size of craft and the windstrength. The stronger the wind the easier it is to right a cat.

7   Lean backwards on the line until your body is almost horizontal to the water (the second crewman may need to assist initially to start the righting of the boat). As the mast breaks the

surface the wind will help the boat come upright. You will find that the momentum created by the boat righting itself can easily capsize it onto the other side. To prevent this one of you should help start the righting procedure, then move to where

◆   Climb onto the lower hull and stand near the bow to submerge it and bring the boat round with the mast pointing into the wind.

◆   Stay under the boat as it flips upright, and make sure it does not capsize the other way.

the lower hull and main beam meet and add your weight to the underside of the beam to stop it flipping up and over.

8 As the boat flips upright both of you will end up under the boat, inside the hulls, holding onto the main beam. This is a good safe position which will stop the boat capsizing the other way and will keep you in good contact with the boat, which may try to sail off.

9 Once the boat is righted you may be able to climb aboard in front of the main beam, but if you have capsized a number of times and are feeling tired make your way under the trampoline to the stern of the boat. Hold the rear beam, push the rudders over to force the boat into the wind and climb aboard between the rear beam and tiller connecting bar (the hull buoyancy is low here and it is much easier to climb aboard).

10 Once you are both safely aboard stow away any loose lines, re-rig the mainsheet, traveller and jibsheet and sail away – perhaps a little wiser for the experience!

◆ Release the mainsheet, jibsheet and traveller to immobilise the boat.

◆ Lean back on the line to pull the boat upright. As the mast clears the water, one of you transfer your weight to the lower hull.

◆ Keep a good grip on the boat in case it tries to sail off without you.

◆ Climb aboard over the rear beam, sort out the boat and get sailing again.

180° CAPSIZE AND RECOVERY

A fully inverted capsize is not a problem
with modern catamarans which have positive
mast buoyancy.

1 Once the boat is totally inverted climb onto
the underside of the trampoline.

2 Make sure the jibsheet, mainsheet and
traveller line are released.

3 Decide which hull is closest to the wind and
position yourself on the downwind hull near the
stern with the righting line coming from the
windward hull.

4 Lean back to raise the windward hull at the
bow and move the mast into a position where it
wants to float to the surface.

5 As the hull becomes 'unstuck' it will quickly
allow the mast to float to the surface and you will
need to move your weight forward to stop the
bow rising.

6 Once the boat is on its side follow the
procedure for a 90° capsize.

This is the normal technique, but some
catamarans can be righted from a full inversion

● Once the boat has passed the point of no return, get
ready to lower yourself into the water; if you delay too
long your weight may well pull the upper hull right over
and turn a simple capsize into a complete inversion.

● The wind is blowing
from left to right.

● Stand on the leeward hull near the
stern to raise the bows.

● The windward bow will rise and the
mast will start to float upwards.

CAPSIZE PROBLEMS

Mistake	Effect
Not grabbing a line as the boat goes over	You lose contact with the boat, which rapidly drifts away – definitely a no go!
Falling into the sail	You may break battens and/or lose contact with the boat
Not turning the boat so the mast points into the wind	The boat is very difficult to right
Not releasing all the control lines	The boat will capsize again or may sail away
Not leaning out fully to right the boat	Difficulty in starting the righting procedure
The crew does not hold on to the lower hull as the boat comes upright	The boat immediately capsizes again the other way

only by standing on the stern of the downwind hull and forcing the bows to point vertically into the air. Then, by moving off the hull and into the water, you can make the boat swing down and lie on its side.

If you lack the physical weight necessary to right an inverted catamaran, get a rescue boat to help start the righting sequence by lifting the mast. In light winds the mainsail can be lowered before following the righting procedure.

☛ As the mast floats towards the surface the windward hull comes clear.

☛ As the boat floats onto its side, get ready to move your weight forward.

☛ Once the boat is on its side, carry on as for a 90° capsize.

Launching and landing

In Part One we concentrated on launching and recovery cross-wind, but in reality this is not always possible. The wind is just as likely to be blowing offshore or onshore and the method for launch or recovery will also depend on the characteristics of your launch area.

Launching with an offshore breeze
To launch safely with an offshore wind float the cat out backwards with the bows pointing into the wind. All sheets and the traveller should be eased right out and the rudders and centreboards (if fitted) should be raised. Position the crew on one hull near the bow to raise the stern out of the water: with the bows acting as a sea anchor the boat will drift out backwards to an area of safe water where the crew can slide onto the trampoline. You then drop the rudders, turn the boat away from the wind and start sailing.

This method is especially useful when you are restricted by other boats. Remember, in all but the lightest airs if you try to sail off a windward shore by simply turning the boat around and heading downwind it will probably sail off without you.

Landing with an offshore breeze
When you are sailing back to a windward shore you will often find the wind very gusty and variable in direction. This is because the air is blowing over the land, around trees, hills and houses. If the landing area is restricted you will need to return to the beach on a beat with your sails sheeted right in. Choose the tack that will give you the most favourable angle back to the beach and raise your leeward rudder and centreboard (if fitted) as you get close. Keep the boat going, or you will lose steerage and the boat will turn onto a reach and gather speed. Release the jib as you approach the shore and use the mainsheet to control your boatspeed. As you get into shallow water point the boat into the wind and lift the windward rudder and centreboard (if fitted). The crew jumps in from the normal place (windward side of the windward hull) and holds on to the bow and bridle wire.

Launching from a leeward shore
With an onshore wind the crew may need to stand in quite deep water to keep the boat afloat with the bows pointing into the wind.

As helmsman, prepare the boat with the traveller pulled in, the jib and mainsheets ready and the centreboards (if fitted) down as far as possible. Choose the tack that gives the most direct line away from the shore.

As crew, hold the windward bow and push the boat away from the wind onto the chosen tack. Climb aboard and immediately sheet in the jib.

Now sail the boat slowly to a safe distance offshore before releasing the sheets and lowering the rudders and centreboards ready for sailing.

◀ The safest way to launch with an offshore breeze is to 'back out' with the sheets eased and the rudders raised.

● Leaving a leeward shore: the crew holds the bow while the helm prepares the sails.

● The crew pushes the bow off the wind and then jumps on.

● Once you are safely off the beach you can drop the rudders.

Landing on a leeward shore

Landing with an onshore breeze needs careful planning because the wind and waves are trying to smash you up on the beach.

In all but the lightest winds it is important to return to the shore under jib alone, as you would in a dinghy. So the first thing to master is the art of lowering the mainsail at sea.

Before you begin, allow for any tidal drift because the jib will only allow you to sail downwind. Now heave-to on *port tack*. (Remember that with the ring and hook halyard lock the boat *must* be on port tack, with the sails blowing over to the starboard side, before the halyard lock will disengage.)

● To lower the main pull on the halyard (left); if you are on port tack the lock will automatically disengage.

● **To land on a leeward shore, start on port tack . . .**   ● **Heave-to by backing the jib . . .**   ● **Lower the main . . .**

Lower the mainsail and store it under the toestraps to prevent the wind getting under it. Then turn the boat downwind and sail under jib alone towards the beach.

Just before you land lift the rudders (and centreboards, if fitted) and release the jib sheet. The crew should be ready to jump over the side, in the normal fashion, and turn the boat back into the wind.

LAUNCH AND RECOVERY IN SURF

In some cases you may have to launch or recover from a beach with surf running. This demands a slightly different technique.

Launching from a lee shore in surf
Get the boat ready to sail with the crew holding the bow. Pick the tack that takes you off the beach most directly and choose a time when the waves are not too big (waves come in sets). When you decide to go, tell the crew to push the bow away from the wind and immediately sheet in the main and jib to give maximum power to the sails. Drive the boat off on a close reach,

pointing slightly into the waves as they approach the boat. Boatspeed is paramount: you cannot afford to be turned sideways or the surf will soon capsize you, while if you are pushed backwards you may damage the rudders on the beach. When you are off, and in sufficient depth, drop your rudders fully; remember that between the waves the water can be quite shallow.

Landing on a lee shore in surf
The most efficient way of returning to a lee shore in surf is to sail in line with the wave pattern straight up the beach. This may sound a little extreme but the options of turning into the wind or coming in under jib alone will lead to far worse problems.

Prepare the boat early, outside the surf break line. Release the mainsail downhaul to depower the sail. Move all crew weight to the back of the boat and choose an area to land on.

Turn the boat downwind and on a line with the surf. Keep sailing at a speed that gives you good steerage. Raise the centreboards (if fitted). As you approach the beach the rudders should trigger automatically; if you do not have this system you will need to send the crew back to

● Sail downwind under jib alone . . .

● Raise the rudders while the crew gets ready to jump ashore.

● And you're there.

the stern to lift the leeward rudder while you carry on steering. When the boat slides onto the beach ease the sails, jump off and turn the boat into the wind as quickly as possible.

● If you have to land on a lee shore in surf prepare early and move your weight to the back of the boat to raise the bows clear of the beach.

PART THREE:

RACING

Race tuning

Initially boat tuning is not as important as learning to sail the boat. It is only when your are looking for that extra five per cent of speed that you need to tune.

Tuning involves making adjustments to the boat, within class rules, to increase its speed. Depending on the class this can range from expensive modifications such as buying different sails and replacing substantial gear to small alterations to the mast rake and sheeting angle, which are 'built into the boat' and cost nothing.

Strict one-designs
Strict one-design catamarans are those which must be sailed as supplied by the builder. Usually all the normal tuning adjustments such as mast rake and sheeting angle are permitted, but the rules do not allow individual interpretation or expensive new equipment. This ensures good class racing at minimum cost and usually supports good second-hand boat values.

◆ **The Tornado is a restricted one-design: although basically identical, each boat is equipped to suit the preferences of its crew.**

Restricted one-design
Restricted boats have rules that are fairly flexible and allow a personal choice in quite a few aspects of the boat.

Open class
This class has very large tolerances in all areas, allowing considerable scope for different hull shapes, sail areas etc. The craft in this class are for the enthusiast who wants to experiment, has ideas and, normally, lots of money. The boats quickly become out-of-date and therefore the second-hand values are normally low.

BASIC TUNING CONTROLS

The principal adjustments that can be made to all boats (including strict one-designs) are as follows:
- Mast rake
- Rig tension
- Batten tension
- Jib fairlead position
- Jib luff tension

- Mainsail luff tension
- Vang (kicking strap) tension
- Spanner line

Mast rake

The rake of the mast is the amount by which it leans forwards or backwards from the upright position. Forward rake gives the boat leeward helm; that is, by moving the centre of effort forward the boat will try to turn away from the wind, which is not something any discerning sailor wants! By leaning the mast back the centre of effort moves back and the boat will turn up towards the wind.

The rake on the mast also effects the trim of the boat, pushing it down at the bow when it is raked forward and down at the stern when raked back.

Ideally, rake the mast so there is a *gentle* pull on the tiller extension when you are beating, with the boat trimmed properly.

Rig tension

A tight rig (shrouds and forestay) which does not allow the mast to move (except to rotate) will ensure you get maximum power from the sails. A loose rig which allows the mast to lean sideways will depower the rig in strong winds. Another disadvantage of a loose rig is that the mast and sails bang around in light winds or choppy sea conditions.

Diamond shrouds are fitted to some catamarans to help control the bend of the mast sideways. They can be tightened to stiffen the mast and power up the main, or loosened to allow the mast to twist away and flatten the mainsail.

Batten tension

A catamaran sail is curved in cross-section like a bird's wing. The curve, or camber, can be increased and decreased by altering the batten tension, and by altering the downhaul tension on the luff of the mainsail (see below).

The more tension in the battens the fuller the sail and the better it is suited to moderate winds. With less tension the sail becomes flatter and better suited to strong and light winds.

Whatever your decision on the day make sure the tension is even throughout, giving an even camber along the mainsail. In extreme conditions the top few battens can be slackened off more than the lower ones to induce twist at the top of the main.

➥ Lace the battens tight for medium winds. This will put plenty of camber in the sail for maximum power.

➥ Loosening them off will both depower the sail for strong winds and make it more efficient in light airs.

Jib fairlead position

The position of the jib fairlead controls the shape
of the jib. If the fairlead is forward the jib is full
and has a tight leech (back edge). This gives a
narrow slot between the jib and main, which
works well in medium winds.

   With the fairlead aft the slot is opened and the
jib is flattened, both effects being good in light
and in strong winds. As a starting point, position
the fairlead as shown in the diagram.

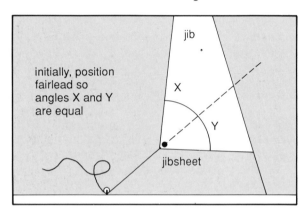

⬆ The fairlead is adjusted in its track with a
screwdriver.

⬇ With the fairlead
forward the jib has a tight
leech and a slack foot.

⬇ Moving the fairlead aft gives a slack
leech and a tight foot, but it does open
the leech for strong winds.

⬇ With the fairlead at the midway point
as shown in the diagram the sail is set up
to suit most conditions.

Jib luff tension

The luff tension on the jib is crucial to the boat's pointing ability because it controls the shape of the forward part of the sail. In light winds you will need minimal luff tension to keep the maximum fullness in the jib one-third of the way aft, but as the wind increases this fullness gets blown backwards towards the leech unless the luff tension is increased. To set the tension on land, pull in the mainsheet as you plan to when sailing. This tightens the forestay. Now tighten the jib downhaul until the luff is *almost* as tight as the forestay.

Mainsail luff tension

The mainsail downhaul controls the fullness of the mainsail. Enough tension is needed to give the sail shape but thereafter the amount depends on the wind strength: the stronger the wind, the more the fullness of sail gets blown back towards the leech. So in strong winds tighten the luff to keep the maximum curve in the most efficient position – one-third of the way aft (from luff to leech).

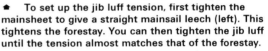

To set up the jib luff tension, first tighten the mainsheet to give a straight mainsail leech (left). This tightens the forestay. You can then tighten the jib luff until the tension almost matches that of the forestay.

♣ With the main downhaul slack there is little camber in the sail and very little power is generated: the boat is effectively 'out of gear' (left). Tightening the downhaul puts camber and power into the sail (right).

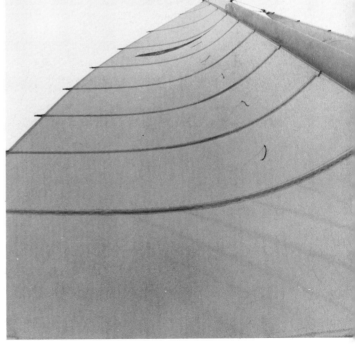

It is a good idea to turn your catamaran on its side on the beach, support the mast and experiment with various tensions. Observe the changes in sail shape: putting on more luff and sheet tension flattens the sails, while more batten tension makes the sails fuller.

Vang (kicking strap)
Vang tension helps reduce mainsail twist on a catamaran with a boom. In strong winds the leech will try to blow open and you will need more vang tension.

Spanner line
The spanner line controls the mast rotation: the tighter the line, the less the mast rotates. If the class rules allow, adjust the spanner line so the mast lines up with the leeward side of the mainsail.

◆   If the spanner line is too tight the mast will not rotate and the leading edge profile will be poor.

◆   ◆   If the mainsheet tension is excessive it will hook the leach on the beat (left). The correct sheet tension gives a smoother, more efficient profile (right).

◆   By dropping the traveller and leaving the sheet as is, you retain the efficient sail shape for the reach.

◆   With the correct spanner line tension the mast swivels to give a rounded, effective leading edge.

♠ If you keep the traveller high on the reach, but slacken the mainsheet, you will get too much twist in the sail.

♠ Maintaining mainsheet tension and lowering the traveller controls the twist and improves performance.

	LIGHT WINDS	MEDIUM WINDS	STRONG WINDS
Jib luff tension	slack	medium	tight – almost as tight as forestay
Mainsail luff tension	just enough to shape the mainsail	enough to give the sail a good curve and prevent creases from the battens when the sheet is pulled in	maximum
Battens	slack – to flatten the sail and allow air to pass over it as quickly as possible	tight – to give maximum camber	reduce tension to flatten the sail and depower the top of the rig

The race

Having made sure your boat is up to scratch, the rest is up to you! The following pages will give you a basic knowledge of the Racing Rules, and enough advice on tactics and strategy to keep you well up with the pack.

THE COURSE

Courses will vary at individual clubs but the standard Olympic-style courses used at most championships and open meetings consist of 'triangle' and 'sausage' legs with a set number of rounds.

In catamaran sailing the wing mark is always set to allow a close reach followed by a broad reach, rather than two broad reaches.

THE RULES

A full discussion of the rules is outside the scope of this book. For the cautious beginner, a few key rules will keep you out of trouble in most cases.

Boats meeting on opposite tacks
A boat is either on a port tack or a starboard tack. It is on a port tack if the wind is blowing over its port side. In the diagram, A, B and C are on port tack; D, E and F are on starboard tack.

A port tack boat must keep clear of a starboard tack boat.

D, E and F have right of way over A, B and C, who must keep clear.

Boats meeting on the same tack
If the boats are overlapped (if the bow of the following boat is ahead of a line at right angles to the stern of the leading boat), then:

A windward boat shall keep clear of a leeward boat.

So G must keep clear of H, I must keep clear of J and L must keep clear of K.

A boat clear astern shall keep clear of a boat clear ahead.

M is overtaking and is not allowed to sail into the back of N.

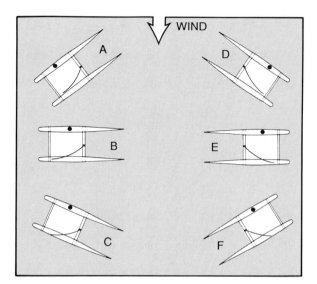

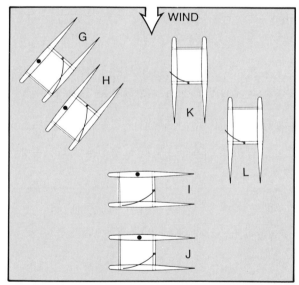

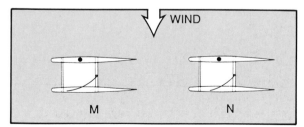

Boats meeting at marks

When two or more boats approach a mark the outside boat must give room to the overlapped boat on the inside. This overlap must be established before the leading boat enters the imaginary two-boat circle around the mark.

When boats are beating towards a mark on opposite tacks this rule does not apply; port gives way to starboard. But for boats about to round the leeward mark on a run port and starboard is irrelevant: the outside boat must give the inside one room to round and, if necessary, to gybe.

PENALTIES

Obviously we all make mistakes! If you tangle with another boat decide whether or not you were in the right. If you consider it was your mistake you must retire or, if the race instructions allow, complete two full circles (a 720° turn) as soon as possible on that leg of the course.

If you feel the other boat is at fault but the other crew disagree with you, launch a protest immediately by flying a small red flag in a conspicuous position on the boat. This will be noted by the committee boat and a protest meeting will be held after the race to hear each boat's story and decide who was in the right.

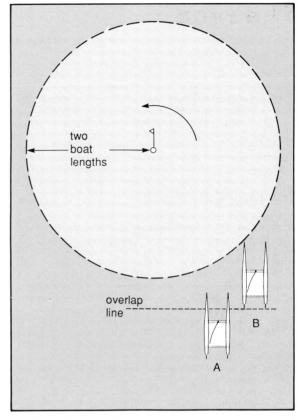

♠ Boat A has established an overlap on boat B before they have reached the two-boat-length circle around the mark. This means that B must give room for A to round the mark.

THE START

The start is the most important part of the race. If you get a bad start, you have to overtake everyone to win – while you're battling past the opposition, the leaders are sailing further ahead. If you get a good start, you're sailing in clear air.

How is a race started?
Most races are started on a beat. The race committee sets an (imaginary) start line, usually between the masts of the committee boat (A) and a buoy (B). They often lay another buoy (C), which does not have to be on the line. Boats are not allowed to sail between C and A.

Ten minutes before the start the class flag (or a white shape) is raised on the committee boat and a gun is fired.

Five minutes before the start the blue peter (or a blue shape) is raised and a gun is fired.

At the start, both flags are lowered (or a red shape is raised) and a gun is fired.

Boats must be behind the start line when the starting gun is fired. Your aim is to be just behind the line, sailing at full speed, when the gun fires.

How can I get a good start?
Set your watch at the ten-minute gun, and check it at the five-minute gun.

During the last few minutes, avoid the 'danger' areas X and Y. From X you cannot get on to the start line because the boats to leeward have right of way. Boat D, for example, will be forced the wrong side of buoy C. In Y you are bound to pass the wrong side of buoy B. Boat F has this problem.

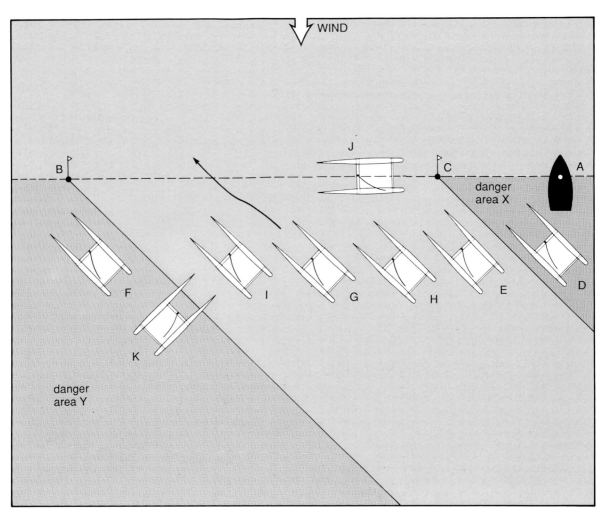

A catamaran will 'sit' quietly on starboard without moving forward much but will drift sideways appreciably. Decide where you want to start and, with about four minutes to go, position yourself several lengths to the right of the spot where you want to be at the gun, on starboard, with your sails flapping. If necessary, back the jib to stop. Try to 'hang' in the same position, using the sails to control your boatspeed, and try to be about three boat lengths behind the start line 10-15 seconds before the gun.

In the last 10-15 seconds bring the boat up to full speed to cross the line immediately after the start gun.

All this is easier said than done, as all the other boats will be attempting to do the same thing. In particular, watch out for leeward boats which are allowed to luff boats to windward: luff early yourself to keep a gap between you. G must keep clear of I but may luff H.

Boats that arrive at the start line too early (J) cannot bear away down the line into boats starting correctly (G), and any boat starting on port (K) must give way to the starboard boats.

When you become more experienced you may try starting on port yourself, as it saves one tack later on. However, it is not recommended for the beginner.

STARTING TECHNIQUE

1 Decide on your starting position
2 Listen for the 10-minute gun, and set your stopwatch
3 Practise crossing the line
4 Check your watch at the 5-minute gun
6 Keep clear of luffing boats to leeward
7 Increase your speed just before the start gun
8 Go for speed after the start.

THE BEAT

After the tension of the start, it's important to settle down and concentrate on sailing hard and fast.

What about other boats?

A boat when beating casts a 'wind shadow'. It also creates an area of disturbed air to windward owing to the wind being deflected by the sail. What's more the air behind the boat is also badly disturbed.

You should therefore avoid sailing just to windward of another boat, behind it or in its wind shadow. In the diagram, boat B should either tack or bear away to clear its wind. Boats D and F should both tack.

Which way should I go?

You may have to modify your course to take account of tides and windshifts, but your first aim should be to make reasonably long tacks to start with, shortening them as you approach the windward mark.

Stay inside the lay lines – these are the paths you would sail when beating to hit the windward mark.

Don't sail into the area beyond the lay lines – if you do, you will have to reach in to the buoy and will lose valuable time and distance.

For safety's sake arrange your tacks so that you come into the mark on starboard tack. This gives you right of way over boats approaching on port tack, and this could be very useful when you meet at the mark.

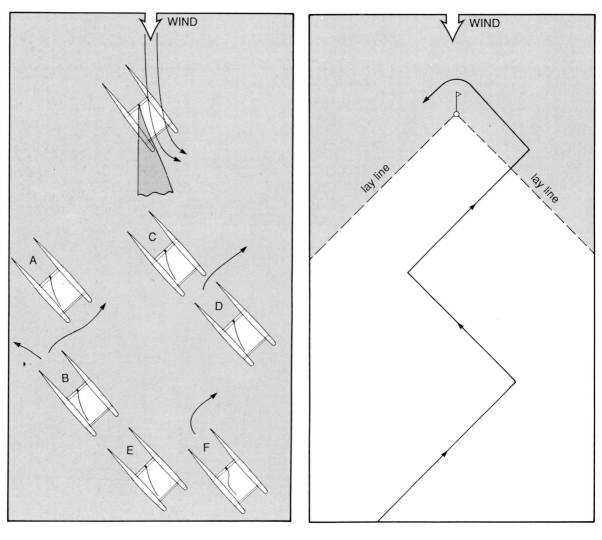

Windshifts

Once you are confident at beating and can tack efficiently, you are ready to start using windshifts.

The wind constantly alters in direction about its mean. Some of the shifts are more pronounced and last longer than others – it is these that you have to spot and use.

In shifty winds, don't go too far from the middle of the beat. Tack if the wind heads you (forces you to alter course *away* from the mark). In the left-hand diagram the boat takes no account of windshifts. Note how little progress it makes compared with the boat in the right-hand diagram which tacks on each major windshift.

The main problem is to differentiate between a real shift and a short-lived change in the wind. For that reason, sail on into each shift for a good distance to make sure it's going to last. If it does, tack.

If you find yourself tacking too often, or if you get confused, sail on one tack for a while until you're sure what the wind is doing. Remember that you lose many boat lengths each time you tack, so there has to be a good reason to do so.

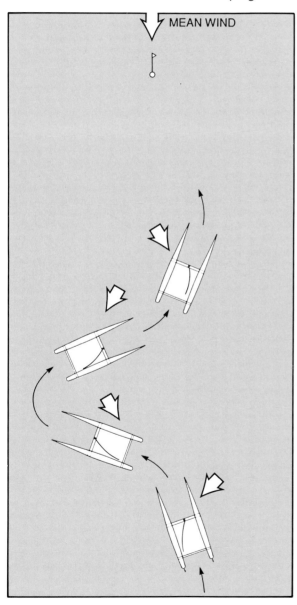

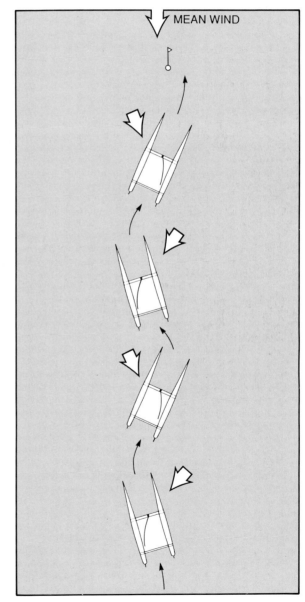

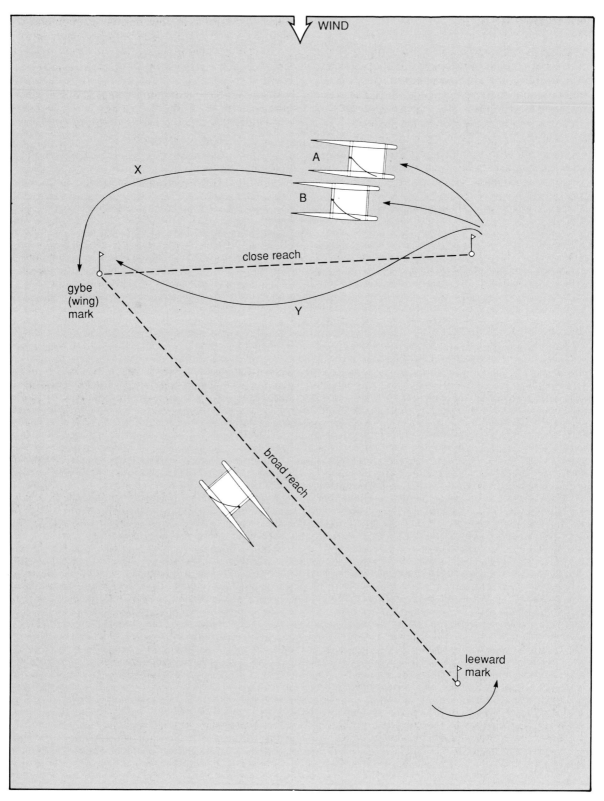

WIND

A

B

X

close reach

gybe
(wing)
mark

Y

broad reach

leeward
mark

THE CLOSE REACH

The quickest way down the reach is a straight line from one mark to the next. However, if your rivals let you sail this course, you're lucky! The problem is that overtaking boats (A) push up to windward. The boats to leeward (B) get nervous about their wind being stolen and steer high also. The result is that everyone sails an enormous arc (X) and arrive at the mark on the run, both of which cause them to lose ground on the leaders.

You have to decide whether or not to go on the 'great circle'; the alternative is to sail a leeward path (Y). You have to go down far enough to avoid the blanketing effect of the boats to windward – but usually you will sail a shorter distance than they do. You will also get the inside turn at the gybe mark. You can go for the leeward route on the second reach too, but this time you will be on the outside at the turn.

Overtaking on the reach
Although it is possible to overtake to leeward you must drop well downwind to avoid your rival's windshadow. Usually it is better to pass to windward, keeping a good boat length clear so that he cannot block you by luffing.

If he does luff, you must respond to avoid a collision. He can continue to luff until you, the helmsman, sitting in your normal position and sighting abeam, come level with his mast. At this point you can call 'Mast abeam' and he must return to his normal course and allow you to pass.

If you are the person who is being overtaken, you must decide whether it is better to protect your position by luffing or allow the faster boat through and not waste time.

ROUNDING THE WING MARK

As you approach the wing mark try to make sure no one has an overlap on you as you enter the two-boat-length circle. Set your traveller and initiate the gybe, starting wide of the mark and finishing close. If someone does have an inside overlap you must give him sufficient room to effect his own gybe.

BROAD REACH

This is similar to the close reach, but sail it with the traveller further out. Be careful not to go too far upwind in protecting your wind from those behind because you will then be forced to approach the next mark on a run.

ROUNDING THE LEEWARD MARK

As you approach the leeward mark again, try to stop anyone obtaining an overlap within the two-boat-length circle. Take the mark wide, but come in close as you sheet in to start the beat. Adjust the controls fluently: traveller first (you may like your crew to pull this in for you) followed by mainsheet and jibsheet together as you steer the boat up towards the wind. Make sure you do not stall by sailing too close; this will make the jib back and the boat will lose speed.

BACK ON THE WIND: BEATING

This will be the second time you have sailed up this part of the course, and hopefully the fleet will have spread out this time. On the first beat you should have been watching the other boats to see which side paid off – if you were watching, you can capitalise on that by choosing a good route this time.

Just as before, try to approach the windward mark on starboard. This time you are going to turn and go downwind to the leeward mark so ease the jib, mainsheet and traveller, and bear away until the bridle wire wind indicator is at 90° to the boat. Decide on your zig-zag course downwind, taking into account any extra puffs of wind you can see on the water. Other boats will also be tacking downwind, so remember the port and starboard rule.

As you approach the leeward mark you will be finishing the first round of the course. If you arrive at the mark on port remember that any boat coming in on starboard has right of way. If you arrive at the mark on starboard, you may have right of way but you will also have to gybe and sheet in before you can sail to windward.

THE FINISH

After the correct number of rounds you will be expected to finish! The finish line is normally set just to windward of the windward mark and consists of a buoy and a finishing boat.

   As you sail up the final beat, decide whether you can overtake the boat in front. If not, concentrate on covering the boat behind by staying between him and the finish.

WELL DONE!

After you have crossed the line pat your crew/helmsman on the back. Don't worry if you weren't the first to finish; you weren't the only one. At a later date think about the race and try to analyse your good and bad decisions so that next time you are better prepared.

Boat care

Most modern catamarans are made of reinforced fibreglass (G.R.P.) so there is no time-consuming varnishing or painting required. However, a catamaran is a fast, high-tech machine that requires regular checking and general care, as would a fast car.

On a daily basis check that:
● The hulls are empty of water, and the bungs are in.
● All circlips are in good condition and taped.
● The trampoline is tight.
● Battens are de-tensioned after the day's sailing.
● The boat and fittings are washed down with fresh water.

Every month, check that:
● The standing rigging shackles are done up tight.
● The rudder assembly is in full working order (it knocks out on hitting an underwater obstruction). Check the pintles and gudgeons.
● All jamming cleats and blocks are running freely.
● Any gelcoat damage is repaired.
● Ropes, toe loops and toe straps are in good condition.
● Wires, rigging and 'eye splices' are not strained, broken or brittle.

Liberal use of WD40 or similar on a monthly basis will make ensure you have easy-to-use free-running equipment and make your sailing far more enjoyable.

STORAGE

If you are storing the boat outside, remember that the mast and hulls have a huge windage. Tie the boat down with wire or ground screws to stop it blowing away in a gale.

◆ If you leave your boat rigged in the boat park, be sure to tie it down securely.

It is a good idea to invest in a hull cover to keep the sun off the decks and trampoline, prolonging their life and preventing fading.

At the end of the season break the boat down into its two hulls, repair any gelcoat damage and store them upside down in a sheltered position or hang them by the beam boxes on the side of a garage or shed.

The sails should be washed and stored in a dry place ready for next year. Standing and running rigging should be checked for straining around the eye splices, washed, dried and stored.

TRAILING AND CAR TOPPING

Boats up to 2.5m (8ft) wide can be trailed in one piece on most UK and European roads. Craft wider than this need to be broken down for trailing or tilted at an angle to reduce the overall width.

Alternatively, smaller catamarans can be carried on the roof of the car using a standard roof rack. A two-piece mast will allow you to tow a trailer or caravan behind if you want.

PART FOUR:

GENNAKERS & TWIN-WIRING

Gennakers

Your cat may have been specifically designed to carry a gennaker, or you may have a 'bolt on' accessory kit. Either way, you need to set up the gear and the rig properly for smooth running and maximum performance.

BOAT PREPARATION

Start by taping up anything that might snag the gennaker. Shorten the mainsail battens to the minimum, and round the free edges.

Add a downwind indicator to help you 'see' changes in apparent wind. Site it carefully or it will foul the sheets or the sail itself.

◆ Tape all sharp edges.

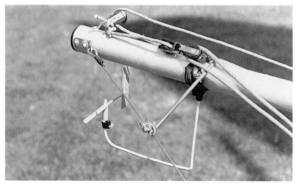

◆ A downwind indicator.

The sail
The gennaker is primarily for downwind sailing, and is designed to produce power and lift. The material is light, has minimum water absorption properties and low stretch characteristics.

If it is cut full (a large belly) it is more powerful downwind and less effective across the wind. The front edge (the luff) is designed to roll (collapse) one third of the way down its length; simply ease the sheet until the luff starts to roll.

If the sail is cut flat you can sail closer to the wind with it, but it is more sensitive to the luff collapsing, making it harder to set. It is not so effective downwind.

Attaching the head
Attach the gennaker's head to the halyard with a shackle, bowline or swivel. Tie a stopper knot about six inches along the halyard to prevent the head being drawn into the halyard block near the top of the mast.

Attaching the clew
There are two ways of attaching the sheets. The first way is to attach both ends to the clew

◆ Attach the head with a bowline.

◆ The stopper prevents the sail being wound into the halyard block.

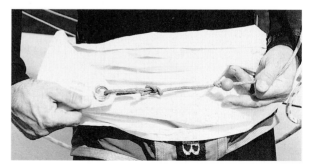

▲ Attaching the sheets to the clew.

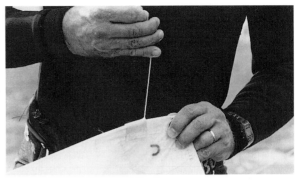

▲ Adjusting the luff line tension.

eye with a bowline, giving a continuous system. The second involves sewing a shackle mid way along the sheet, then knotting each end on the trampoline. (This is useful if the gennaker is recovered by hand.)

Choose sheets to be non-absorbent, thick enough to hold in a range of conditions, and in a different colour from the other sheets.

Attaching the tack

Secure the tack to the outhaul line at the end of the pole. Again it is advisable to have a stopper knot or plastic ball to prevent the tack being pulled into the block.

The luff line

Stretch the luff loosely between two people and adjust the luff line to be marginally tighter than the luff tape. This prevents the tape stretching.

Clearance elastics

Use elastic 'ties' to stop the sail or halyard hooking round the hounds, diamond spreaders, the lower diamond tensioners, or any other projections.

Hoist the gennaker ashore to check all the lines are led outside everything.

↓ Clearance elastics at the hounds (left) diamond spreaders (centre) and lower diamond tensioner (right).

● Use the 'hand twist' method to check the luff tension.

Checking the hoist

Prevention is better than cure, so whenever possible carry out a dry land hoist to confirm that everything is correct: all halyards and lines are on the outside and running smoothly.

Next, check the sail's luff tension when fully hoisted. A good starting guide is to hold the luff edge in your hand and then just be able to rotate your hand through 180°, wrapping the sail around your knuckles. Too much luff tension will destroy the sail shape, too little and you will have difficulty in setting the gennaker correctly.

The luff length depends on the distance from the end of the gennaker pole to the halyard block near the top of the mast, so if you change the mast rake or pole height this will affect the luff tension and you will need to reset the luff.

Stow the gennaker neatly, preferably on the leeward side for your first hoist. Tidy and secure the gennaker sheets to prevent their being washed overboard.

POLE TENSION

Depending on the length and size of the pole, a series of bridle wires are used to support its length. The wires attached to the outboard end

● Hoisting to leeward: Here we go.

● Pre-bend in the pole helps keep it straight when the tension comes on.

control the height and restrain the sideways pull. Mid-pole bridle wires help prevent the middle of the pole flexing under gennaker load. For light and thin poles, I recommend pre-bend to stiffen the pole. Also, don't use the pole end as a trolley handle when launching!

YOUR FIRST SAIL WITH A GENNAKER

I recommend Force 2 for your first attempt.

● Sail upwind to give yourself sea room, and check the area you're about to sail into.
● Bear away onto the tack which allows the gennaker to be hoisted on the leeward side.

● Pull the halyard fast.

FIRST SAIL: *DO'S*

Do check all edges are taped

Do check the lines before going afloat.

Do practice the hoist and recovery on land first.

Do keep watch for other craft.

Do communicate with each other during hoisting, recovery and course changes.

FIRST SAIL: *DON'TS*

Don't raise the gennaker on a reach.

Don't raise the gennaker without having sea room.

Don't pass other craft to windward without leaving a gap for bearing away.

Don't leave insufficient room for recovering the sail and preparing for upwind sailing.

Don't try to gybe too quickly.

Don't release the halyard before the recovery line or clew is under tension, ready to be recovered.

- Set the daggerboards (if fitted), jib and mainsail for downwind sailing.
- Raise the gennaker with the boat heading a few degrees below your normal downwind course.
- Once the sail is fully hoisted, bring in the mainsail traveller about half way. Head up to just above the 45° downwind sailing angle, and pull in the gennaker sheet.
- Lock on to the downwind power, then bear away using the apparent wind created.
- Experiment with the downwind sailing angle, the speed at which the apparent wind is generated, and how the potential sailing angle can change.
- Now experiment with a steady gybe giving the crew time to adjust his position and sheets.
- For your first drop bear away downwind, recover the gennaker to leeward and stow it.

HOISTS AND DROPS

In this section I will show you a variety of ways to hoist and drop the gennaker, and how to sail with it on a reach and a run.

Hoisting to leeward

Raising to leeward is the fastest and most convenient hoist. The sail is immediately positioned on the correct side of the boat, which can be brought up to speed smoothly and efficiently.

- Bear away to just below the normal downwind sailing angle.

If at any time you feel out of control, bear away and sail deeper downwind, if necessary recovering the gennaker earlier than expected.

☛ **Set the sail.**

☛ **Power away.**

◆ Dropping to windward: preparation.

◆ Pull the windward sheet.

HOISTING TO LEEWARD: *DO'S*

Do check the leeward area before hoisting

Do hoist the sail before pulling out the outhaul.

HOISTING TO LEEWARD: *DON'TS*

Don't hoist on a reach

Don't sheet in before the gennaker is fully hoisted.

- Adjust the other controls for downwind sailing: downhaul, mast rotation, jib angle, sheets, main outhaul etc.
- Check the area to leeward.
- Hoist the gennaker (halyard first, if separate from the outhaul) as fast as possible to prevent the sail touching the water.
- Once fully hoisted, head up to bring the apparent wind indicator 90 degrees across the boat.
- Adjust the gennaker and mainsail sheets, power up and alter your course to the induced apparent wind direction.

The windward hoist

This is best avoided because it's slow and also because you need to point the boat well downwind before the hoist to allow the gennaker to blow across the front of the forestay.

However, you may be forced into a windward hoist through bad planning – ie you didn't think ahead on the previous drop!

Firstly, get the boat ready by bearing away and by setting the daggerboards, the downhaul and the outhaul. The crew pulls up the gennaker fast on the halyard; the helmsman can encourage the clew to blow across the forestay by initially heading downwind and then by luffing up a little. Finally, set the sail by pulling in the sheet, after which the helmsman can come up to his proper course.

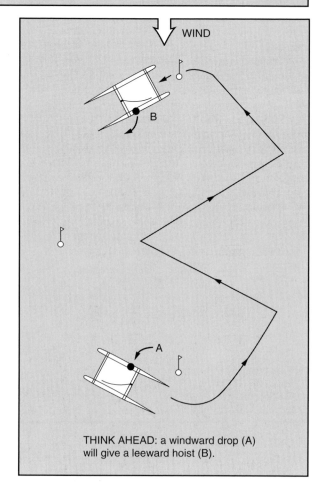

THINK AHEAD: a windward drop (A) will give a leeward hoist (B).

↑　**Recover the gennaker.**

↑　**Stow it**

WINDWARD HOIST: *DO'S*

● Do check the area to leeward before you bear away.
● Do preset the boat's other equipment.
● Do sail low initially.
● Do hoist fast.
● Do make sure the helmsman heads up at the right moment to get the gennaker to blow across the forestay.
● Do use clearance elastics to prevent the gennaker snagging.
● Do make sure the sheets are free, or the gennaker will fill with wind during the hoist.

WINDWARD HOIST: *DON'TS*

● Don't hoist the gennaker to windward on a reach because it will blow into the jib and snag.
● Don't stay on the run too long or the gennaker will wrap itself around its own luff.
● Don't let the sheet snag or the gennaker will fill with wind too early.

LOWERING THE GENNAKER

A windward drop is preferable because the crew is positioned on the windward side of the boat and can see what's going on. There is also less chance of the gennaker being sucked along the leeward side of the mainsail and snagging on the main's battens during the drop. Most courses involve rounding marks to port, so a windward drop sets up the gennaker for a leeward hoist next time.

The windward drop

Since you are going to bear away, check the area to leeward. Bear away and pull the windward gennaker sheet to pull the clew of the sail around the forestay and back to your hand. Throw off the halyard (the friction in the system will prevent the sail falling in the water) and pull the gennaker down alongside the mast using the leech. Pull it as fast as you can so it makes a bundle on the forward part of the trampoline. Finally, stuff it into the bag along with the lines and sheets. There is no need to worry about making a neat bundle though try to avoid twists. When all is clear, the helmsman can come back up towards the wind.

TOP TIP When recovering make sure that the gennaker comes in under the jibsheet otherwise

WINDWARD DROP: *PROBLEMS*

Difficulty in bringing the gennaker around to windward.

Halyard becomes tangled at the cleat.

Sail tries to blow into the water between the hulls.

WINDWARD DROP: *SOLUTIONS*

Bear away more and release the leeward sheet.

Prepare earlier to reduce knotting
– stream excess line over the stern.

Release the tack outhaul before dropping the halyard. Recover at a faster rate.

●   **Dropping to leeward: preparation.**

●   **Pull the leeward sheet.**

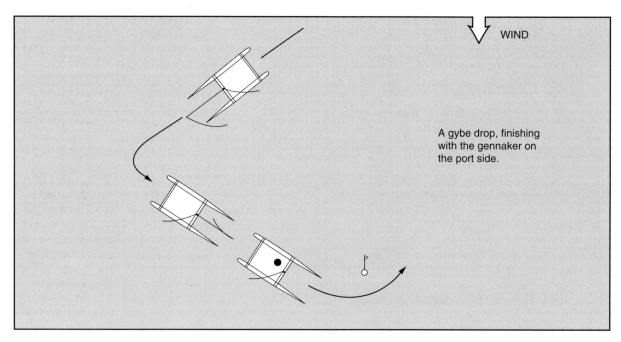

WIND

A gybe drop, finishing
with the gennaker on
the port side.

●   **A gybe drop: preparation.**

●   **Gybe, and sheet in the old gennaker sheet.**

● Recover the gennaker.

● Stow it.

GYBE DROP: *PROBLEMS*

Boat not ready for new leg of the course.

Hull lifts after the gybe.

Halyard knots at cleat.

GYBE DROP: *SOLUTIONS*

Gybe further away from the mark.

Check port jibsheet is released.

Stream over the rear beam prior to drop.

you'll be in a real mess later. Tensioning the windward jibsheet before you begin is a good way to make yourself do this. Alternatively, lay the slack windward sheet over your neck during recovery.

If you practice both a windward and a leeward drop you're in a stronger position when racing because you can choose which to do in order to give yourself a leeward hoist next time.

The leeward drop

The advantage of this drop is that you don't have to pull the sail around to windward. However, it does put the crew on the leeward side, and if the boat is rounding up in any breeze this can lead to a capsize. So it is generally used in light winds or when you are forced to recover the gennaker on a particular side.

Check to leeward, then bear away. Hand the gennaker sheet to the helmsman who can keep

● Recover the gennaker.

● Stow it. Note the rounding is to starboard.

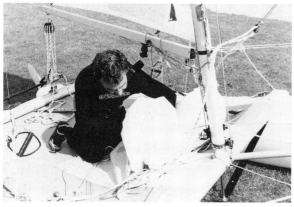

◆ Stowing in a bag.

◆ Packed.

the sail flying. The crew now moves forward and to leeward and grabs the sheet near the clew (and under the jibsheets). Then he/she can release the halyard and pull the sail down beside the mast as fast as possible. Preferably, release the tack after the sail has been lowered to prevent the gennaker or halyard from blowing back along the mainsail.

FOR A LEEWARD DROP: *DO'S*

● Check that the tail of the halyard is free to run, by throwing the whole lot overboard so the speed of the boat pulls it into a straight line. Alternatively, have it suitably coiled in the trampoline bag - although there's seldom time to do this properly.
● Do bear away enough to prevent the sail blowing back and hooking on the battens. If it does, keep downwind until the head of the sail has been recovered.
● As helmsman, do pull in on the sheet to bring the sail within your crew's reach.
● Do pull the sail down as fast as possible.

The gybe drop
This is probably the best and fastest recovery because it enables you to drop the sail to wind-ward without having to bear away and pull it round the forestay first. So, for example, you can come in to the leeward mark on starboard, gybe and pull in the gennaker on the port side ready for a leeward hoist next time. Sounds easy doesn't it?

Actually it is. Coming down to the leeward mark initiate the gybe. The crew dives across to the new windward side, sheeting in the gennaker on the old sheet. This enables him

to grab the clew, throw off the halyard, and bundle the sail down to windward alongside the mast and into the bag.

TOP TIP Before you begin, prepare the boat for the next leg of the course. Don't forget to release the old jibsheet and pull on the new one. The helmsman can handle the dagger-boards while the manoeuvre is in progress.

METHODS OF STORING THE GENNAKER

There are two methods: a bag or a chute.

Storing in a bag
A bag is simple and is currently the most common system, but it does require a lot of

◆ After a drop, secure the halyard and sheets.

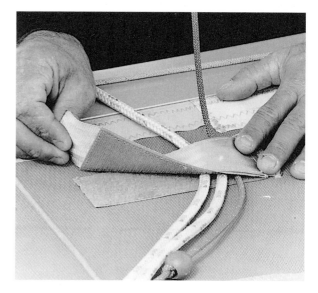

♠   **Lowering into a chute**.

work on the part of the crew. As a result it can be slow.

Another problem is that the halyard and sheets must be stowed carefully or they will pull the sail out of the bag if they are left to drag in the water. So they need a secure holding point. In the photographs, note the velcro strap which keeps the ropes secure.

Storing in a chute
A chute removes a lot of work for the crew and is thus quite a fast system. The disadvantages

are that, because the chute is on one side of the forestay, the sail can only be set and recovered on that side. The system tends to wear the sail, although a good system will have been worked on to reduce friction. Note that the chute is normally rigged on the port side, giving a windward drop and leeward hoist on port hand courses.

To drop with a chute simply bear away, pull the recovery line and relase the halyard, allowing the sail to collect and be pulled down into the chute.

Sailing with the gennaker

In this section we are going to look at how to use the gennaker in a range of conditions, both downwind and reaching.

Let's begin with downwind sailing, because that's where the sail is most effective. Note that in all cases you want to aim for the windward hull to be just clear of the water (obviously you won't achieve this in light airs).

DOWNWIND IN LIGHT AIRS

Crew position
Well forward to lift the transom.

Daggerboards
Pull both daggerboards half to three quarters up.

Mainsail
Set the main with a good degree of twist by putting the traveller near the middle and sheeting off. Rotate the mast 90 degrees, ie across the boat. Ease the outhaul. Apply a small amount of downhaul to twist the top of the sail.

Jib
Roll up the jib.

Sheeting the gennaker
The crew will be well down to leeward, and from his position on the front beam he can see the luff of the gennaker and trim the sheet to keep the telltales flowing or the luff just on the curl.

Technique
The objective is to keep air flowing over the gennaker and power in the sail. This is all about apparent wind: the helmsman steers up and the boat accelerates. He can then bear away gently, trying to sail low while encouraging the new apparent wind to stay attached. If he goes too low the gennaker collapses or at least the tension in the sheets drops and the speed falls. This is the signal to head back up a bit and repeat the process. But the objective is not to let the gennaker collapse! One way round this is for the crew to tell the helmsman all the time how much pressure there is on the sheet. As soon as the pressure begins to fall the helmsman can then decide whether he wants to luff up to generate more speed.

LIGHT AIR: *PROBLEMS*	LIGHT AIR: *SOLUTIONS*
Lack of power in the gennaker.	Head up to attach air flow.
Boat loses direction when steering.	Increase daggerboard depth to create resistance to sideways drift.

☛ On a light wind run roll the jib and sit forward.

☛ Sheet off to put twist in the mainsail. Raise both daggerboards like this. Trim to the luff of the gennaker.

● **Downwind in medium air: head up and sheet in to power up, then bear away.**

DOWNWIND IN MEDIUM AIR

Crew position
The helmsman is to windward but slightly aft of the daggerboard. The crew is to leeward and also slightly aft.

Daggerboards
The leeward one is three quarters up and the windward one is right up. These allow you to bear away quickly if you need to.

Mainsail
Drop the traveller slightly below centre. Mast rotated to 90 degrees across the boat. Enough downhaul to induce a bit of twist. Outhaul on a medium setting.

Jib
Trim to keep the telltales streaming.

Steering technique and sail trim
The helmsman and crew must work together to keep the boat up to speed. Initially head up and sheet in a little to make the boat accelerate. Then turn away from the wind onto a lower course, easing the gennaker to help this. The boat will accelerate further on this new course and the gennaker will need to be trimmed in to compensate. Continue to trim the gennaker to changes in wind strength and boat direction. For example, in a gust of wind the helmsman will bear away and you'll need to ease the sheet to accommodate this, before sheeting in as the boat accelerates.

ON A MEDIUM AIR RUN: *PROBLEMS*	ON A MEDIUM AIR RUN: *SOLUTIONS*
Difficulty in bearing away in gusts.	1. Move crew weight aft. 2. Check that the windward daggerboard is raised. 3. Raise the leeward daggerboard further. 4. Encourage the crew to ease the gennaker during the manoeuvre.
Helm feels twitchy.	Check the twist of the mainsail leech. Set the traveller further outboard and pull in the mainsheet.

Meanwhile, the helmsman will be adjusting the mainsheet and/or the traveller to trim the mainsail to the optimum angle (taking care not to narrow the slot between the two sails). The leech telltales are the best indicator of good mainsheet trim.

DOWNWIND IN A STRONG BREEZE

In strong winds you will need to make much bigger changes in course and sail trim to keep the boat upright. In a gust the helmsman needs to bear away radically or the boat will capsize to leeward. If the gennaker sheet is not eased at the appropriate stage the bow will dig in and the boat may cartwheel forwards.

Crew position
Although the crew may start slightly forward (just aft of the daggerboards) he needs to be ready to move back towards the rear beam, and inboard as required. The helmsman is near the rear beam and to windward.

Daggerboards
Pull both daggerboards right up. This will allow the boat to turn to leeward quickly.

Mainsail
Prevent nosediving by controlling the twist in the leech of the main. To achieve this, set up the mainsail by increasing mainsheet tension and easing the traveller as required. Then steer to this, sailing deeper as needed.

Ease the outhaul slightly. Stop the mast over-rotating and apply some downhaul to keep control of the mast bend above the hounds.

Jib
Set the jib to its telltales.

Technique
In all but the strongest of winds it's fast to have the windward hull just out of the water. The technique is to head up carefully and lock on to the apparent wind, creating a dramatic increase in speed and power. This may cause the windward hull to lift alarmingly. At this point bear away sharply, easing the gennaker sheet considerably and probably the traveller (or mainsheet - whichever you prefer) as well. The helmsman may choose to keep his hand on the traveller line which is his fast-response control, adjusting the mainsheet only for fine tuning. Hammering off in a cloud of spray, keep adjusting the sails and the tiller to the wind conditions and the waves, trying to sail as low as you can while keeping good speed.

The crew is covered in spray and it's hard for him to see what's going on so the helm needs to keep up a running commentary: "Bearing away – ease the sheet" or "Heading up – sheet in".

If it looks as though you are going to capsize to leeward, continue to bear off until things stabilize or even until the boat is going straight downwind. Note that by going fast the pressure on the sails is reduced, making nosediving less of a problem.

USING THE GENNAKER ON A REACH

Although reaching crosswind with the gennaker set is exhilarating, it is essentially a light-to-medium wind technique. In strong winds the boat may develop lots of lee helm (ie you have to push the tiller to keep the boat on course). Often the sideways drift created is more trouble that it's worth, and indeed in a gust you may not be able to bear away quickly enough to prevent a capsize. With the centreboards down (to resist drift), the boat can quickly tip over.

♣ **On a strong wind run head up carefully to increase speed.**

♣ **Bear away sharply....**

♣ **....and power off.**

REACHING IN LIGHT AIRS

Crew position
Both forward and on opposite sides
of the mast.

Daggerboards
The leeward daggerboard should be down, to
resist the pressure to drift sideways, and the
windward daggerboard should be between
down and half up.

Mainsail
Rotate the mast until the spanner bar points at
the leeward shroud. In essence the mast is not
very rotated because the apparent wind is well
forward. The downhaul should be just tight
enough to remove creases and the outhaul
75% out. Put the traveller on the centreline.

➥ **Sheet off to put twist in the mainsail. Move weight
forward. The helmsman steers to the luff of the gennaker.**

Jib
Trim the jib to the telltales.

Technique
As the boat heads up from a broad reach sheet
in the gennaker. Eventually there comes a point
where the sail is simply dragging the boat sideways, creating no forward power. It's important
to identify this point, and mark the sheet where
it comes through the ratchet block.

Once the sheet is trimmed (almost) to this
setting, all the helmsman can do is to steer a
course to maximise boatspeed, reacting to the
apparent wind. There is no point in sheeting in
harder and trying to head higher, as you will
lose speed and increase leeway.

Pre-plan each gennaker reach: you may need
to sail above the layline initially, without the
gennaker, to give an acceptable angle from
which to hoist the gennaker and blast down
the rest of the leg. Alternatively, you can bear
off early with the gennaker up, then drop it
and close reach up to the mark.

LIGHT AIR REACHING: *PROBLEM*

Boat sails sideways.

LIGHT AIR REACHING: *SOLUTION*

Bear away/ease gennaker. Create forward movement
and lift from the daggerboards before luffing up.

◆   **Reaching in medium winds.**   ◆   **Bear away in a gust, easing the gennaker sheet.**   ◆   **Here the boat is back under control.**

REACHING IN MEDIUM AIR

This normally requires twin trapezing – for this technique see later. The trick is to play the gennaker sheet and the mainsheet continuously to keep the boat up to speed. But if she's constantly being overpowered it's more effective to pull on main downhaul rather than sheet out the main too much and close the slot between the main and the gennaker. Pulling on the downhaul twists off and flattens the top of the mainsail, which is above gennaker level.

Crew position
To windward, on and off the trapeze as appropriate and fore and aft as appropriate.

Daggerboards
Have the leeward daggerboard quarter to half up and the windward one half up. This allows you to bear away quickly in a gust, although for good performance in slightly lighter winds you would aim to put more daggerboard down to give you good grip.

Mainsail
The helmsman will need to play the mainsheet and occasionally adjust the downhaul to keep the boat balanced and powered up. Whether you decide to play the mainsheet or the traveller will come from experience.

Jib
Set to the telltales or out a touch more to keep the slot open.

Technique
In a lull, the crew simply comes inboard, trimming the gennaker to the new wind. In a gust you've got to convert the force in the sail into forward speed so bear away, easing the gennaker sheet to allow the boat to accelerate. Finally, come back up, without the windward hull flying too high.

If you're experiencing too much lee helm, try moving crew weight aft. If the load on the gennaker sheet is excessive, try easing the gennaker tack line - this brings the sail further aft, reducing the turning effect.

REACHING IN MEDIUM AIRS: *PROBLEMS*	REACHING IN MEDIUM AIRS: *SOLUTIONS*
Boat trips up when bearing away in a gust.	Raise the leeward daggerboard slightly.
Mainsail needs excessive adjustment.	Pull on more downhaul.
Boat capsizes across the wind.	Bear away earlier to generate forward power.
Gennaker keeps collapsing.	Check luff tension, or sail a lower course.

➥   **Reaching in strong winds.**

➥   **Bear away radically when a gust hits!**

REACHING IN STRONG WINDS

Don't try this at home, folks!

As with all gennaker sailing, you need to steer a course that gives you space to leeward to bear away into when you need it. It's no good overtaking a slower boat closely to windward, for example; if a gust hits as you're passing him you have nowhere to go. The skill of strong wind gennaker reaching is to keep the speed up (which takes the weight out of the wind) and to be able to de-power the rig substantially when needed. Normally you wouldn't carry a gennaker on a strong wind reach, but you may find you are forced to do this if the conditions change.

Crew position
As far out and as far back as you can manage.

Daggerboards
Put the windward daggerboard half way down, and the leeward one between half and three quarters down.

Mainsail
Your objective is to de-power the main as much as possible. Rotate the mast so that the spanner points towards the leeward rear beam housing, and then apply full downhaul and outhaul tensions.
   Take care that the pull from the gennaker block (near the top of the mast) is well supported by good diamond tension and mast rotation.

Jib
Trim the jib so that it's not really doing anything, but is not flapping either.

Technique
In a gust bear away hard and keep going until the speed has built up and you can recover.
   For speed allow the weather hull to rise a little as this helps counteract the lee helm that the gennaker is causing.
   Again, if you need to bear away do so rapidly and make sure that the crew eases the gennaker as you do so.

REACHING IN HEAVY AIRS: *PROBLEMS*	REACHING IN HEAVY AIRS: *SOLUTIONS*
Unable to maintain required course.	Bear away and drop the gennaker.
Mainsail flogging ineffectively.	Bear away/drop gennaker.
Mast starts to 'pant'.	Bear away/drop gennaker.

● **The wild thing: get the windward hull flying.**

● **Bear away, and hold it there.**

THE WILD THING

This is a technique you need to develop for fast downwind sailing in medium and somewhat strong winds with flattish sea conditions.

Start on a broad reach and position your crew to leeward. Encourage the windward hull to fly to about 15-20°: it needs to be high enough that when you bear away it won't flop down again but not so high that the boat starts to skid sideways.

As the boat builds up speed bear away (you'll be forced to anyway) in a smooth but determined fashion, keeping the hull flying and the crew down to leeward (but he may also have to move aft depending on the wind and waves).

If at some stage the wind dies, you'll need to head back up again to keep the hull flying, constantly adjusting the main and gennaker.

The effect of the Wild Thing is that the boat accelerates downwind very fast, because there is only the resistance of one hull in the water. The apparent wind goes ahead and you are able to sail still lower: significantly lower and faster than someone who is not doing the Wild Thing.

THE WILD THING: *PROBLEMS*	THE WILD THING: *SOLUTIONS*
Unable to raise a hull without coming up too high towards the wind.	1. Insufficient wind. 2. Lower leeward daggerboard.
Unable to bear away efficiently.	1. Move crew weight aft. 2. Raise leeward daggerboard further.
Boat stalls when bearing away.	1. Change direction more smoothly. 2. Concentrate on not turning too far downwind.

◆   **Gybing: get ready.**

◆   **Turn..**

◆   **Pull the gennaker across.**

◆   **Power up and bear away.**

GYBING

The secret of gybing is to do it at speed. If you bear away and pussyfoot about, the boat will slow and the sails will load up and when they do come across they will do so with a good deal of pressure behind them.

So build up maximum speed on a broad reach. As you turn into the gybe ease the gennaker sheet until the clew is approximately half way along the jib. Then when you do gybe the gennaker will naturally blow through between the jib and its own luff. If you ease it too far it will wrap around its own luff and if you don't let it out far enough it can hit the jib fair and square and won't blow through, with the possibility of a capsize.

Re-setting the jib during the gybe is of secondary importance, although it's a good idea to release it before you begin.

The helmsman should concentrate firstly on building up speed and secondly on making a smooth turn, helping the main across. After the gybe, head up to lock on to the new apparent wind before bearing away onto the proper course. Note that after a gybe in light winds you will need to come up higher to pick up good speed, while in strong winds strike a balance between speed and control – and indeed if you come up too high you risk a capsize on the new gybe.

GYBING: *PROBLEMS*	GYBING: *SOLUTIONS*
Boat stalls after gybe.	1. Enter with more speed. 2. Luff higher after the gybe.
Boat heels over after the gybe but does not power off.	Ease gennaker once pulled through to the new leeward side.

Technical options

Here I am simulating the effect of moving the gennaker sheet lead: (left) forward, (right) aft.

The purpose of this section is to explain how to use the tuning kit you may find on your boat or may want to add.

Gennaker sheeting angles
Choose the position of the gennaker turning block to get a fair pull on the sail, so that when you sheet in the leech and foot both tighten in unison. Note that you will set this up with one particular mast rake, but if you need to change the rake substantially the clew will obviously move and you will need to make a corresponding adjustment to each turning block's position.

The best way to do this is to sight the leech of the sail ashore, looking at the way it opens and closes during adjustment.

In strong winds you want the leech looser than the foot, to enable the wind to blast out of the sail and pass down a big gap between the gennaker and mainsail. To achieve this, move the gennaker sheet lead aft a bit.

Note that you don't move the lead forward in light airs, because this will only hook the gennaker leech and close the slot between it and the mainsail.

The pull of the gennaker high up the mast needs supporting. The sudden shock loadings transmitted through the gennaker in a gybe or nosedive are best controlled by good mainsheet tension which tightens the mainsail leech and supports the upper mast.

Barber haulers
Barber haulers are a means of on-the-water adjustment to sheeting angles, offering limited control of leech twist and sail slot. By careful adjustment fine tuning of the gennaker sheeting angles can be made relevant to the position of the gennaker and the wind conditions.

HOISTING SYSTEMS
There are three main systems: two-line, one-line and 1:2.

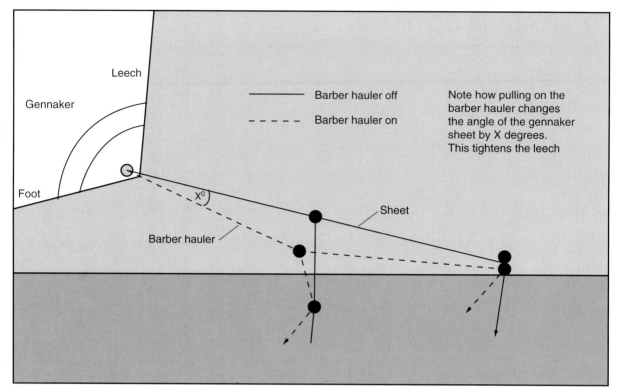

Leech

Gennaker

Foot

—————— Barber hauler off

– – – – – Barber hauler on

Note how pulling on the barber hauler changes the angle of the gennaker sheet by X degrees. This tightens the leech

X^0

Sheet

Barber hauler

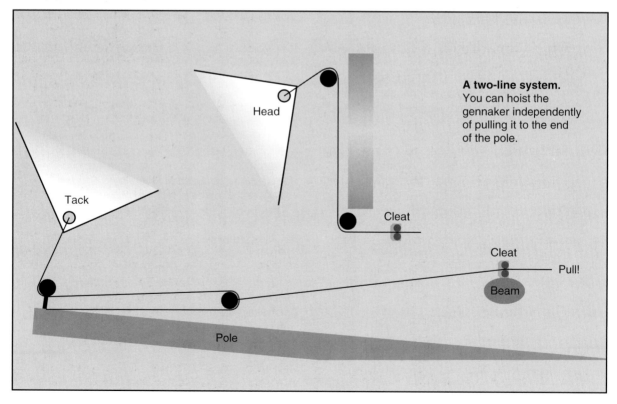

Head

A two-line system.
You can hoist the gennaker independently of pulling it to the end of the pole.

Tack

Cleat

Cleat

Pull!

Beam

Pole

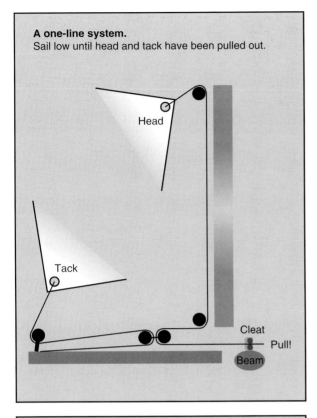

A one-line system.
Sail low until head and tack have been pulled out.

Head

Tack

Cleat

Pull!

Beam

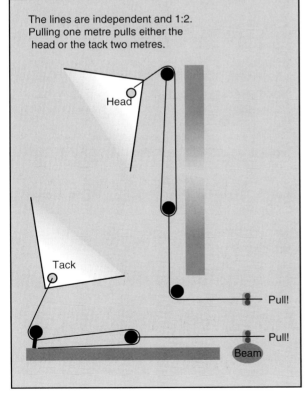

The lines are independent and 1:2.
Pulling one metre pulls either the
head or the tack two metres.

Head

Tack

Pull!

Pull!

Beam

Two-line system

Here you have a separate halyard and a separate gennaker tackline. In essence you can hoist the sail up and out independently. Thus if you hoist first and then pull it to the end of the pole it helps prevent the sail going in the water. Similarly, on the drop you can let the halyard off, keeping the foot of the sail stretched out to the end of the pole. This reduces the chance of the gennaker wrapping round the back of the mainsail during a leeward drop. The disadvantage is, of course, that it is slightly slower to operate and less automatic for the crew.

One-line system

Here, pulling on one line pulls the sail up and also out to the end of the pole. The advantage of this is that it's fast and it's simple to envisage. But it results in an awful lot of line lying around on the trampoline and it has no independent control over the tack and head positions.

1:2 system (2:1 in reverse)

Here, by pulling 1 metre on the halyard the head of the sail rises 2 metres. This means the sail can be pulled up twice as fast, and you have half the amount of rope lying on the trampoline. The only disadvantage is that you have to pull twice as hard! The loadings on the blocks are also quite high. Note that you would normally have 1:2 on the halyard and 1:2 on the tack but they have to be pulled independently because the loadings are so high.

Halyard storage systems

Halyards are an issue on a catamaran. If you do nothing with the loose ends they will eventually snarl up and let you down at a critical moment.

If you leave the halyards loose, the best way to untangle them is to trail them over the rear beam and let the water pull them out straight. Sadly, this doesn't always work and also if you are on port tack a starboard boat has quite a large target (ie the halyard is part of the boat).

Another idea is a spool which winds up the halyard in much the same way that a dog lead works. Good idea, but normally it is only suitable for thin line.

A third system is a shock-cord takeaway system with pulleys, so that the loose halyard is pulled under the trampoline and taken away.

Tactics with the gennaker

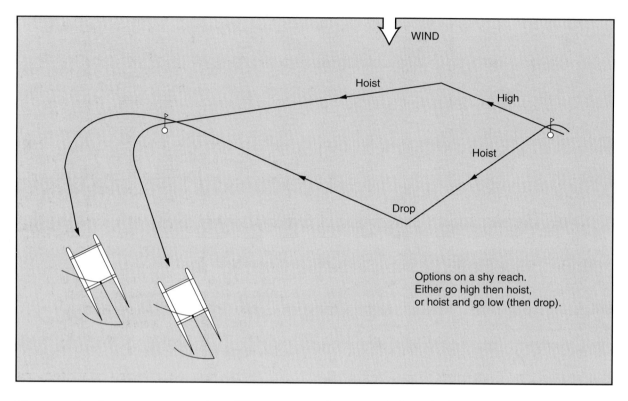

WIND

Hoist

High

Hoist

Drop

Options on a shy reach.
Either go high then hoist,
or hoist and go low (then drop).

The gennaker imposes some rather different tactics and strategies on the racecourse.

ON THE REACH

If you can lay the next mark under gennaker, bang it up and go!

If you can't lay it you have two choices: either sail high initially, hoist and reach to the next mark and gybe around it; or hoist immediately, forcing you to sail low, then drop and close reach to the buoy before gybing and hoisting again on the next leg.

All things being equal the first option is the best because it only requires one hoist and you are more likely to keep clear air during the first leg.

Overtaking to windward on a reach

If you are overtaking to weather, take care because you won't be able to bear away in a gust. Similarly, be very careful about passing close to windward of somebody who isn't flying a gennaker: if he luffs, you are obliged to respond. Keep a good distance to weather and at the opportune moment bear away in a gust.

Overtaking to leeward on a reach

Passing to leeward is difficult without a sufficient gap between the boats to maintain some stability in the wind. Be more ready to bear off in a gust than your opponent, break through and then slowly regain the windward ground you have lost.

ON THE RUN

As you round the windward mark, try to make sure that you don't get trapped to leeward of another boat. Your objective is to keep high after the mark to pick up speed before bearing off, in the way we've been describing. If you have a boat to windward you may get trapped on a low course, unable to accelerate, with the

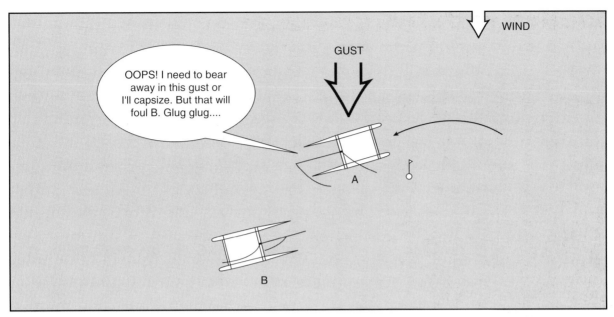

only immediate option of gybing away.

Also, beware of boats still beating up to the mark on port when you are reaching away on starboard. If a gust comes you will need to bear away to avoid a capsize, but the rules say that you must give the port boat room to keep clear and this may just not be possible for him. The solution? Think further ahead.

If there's a downwind gate on the course, I recommend that you go through it on starboard otherwise you may get shut out. Remember: starboard boats sailing upwind have right of way over all boats sailing downwind.

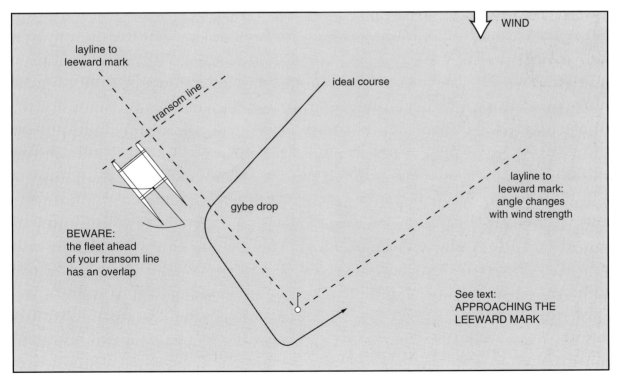

● Basic recovery from a capsize. Make sure your crew is OK.

● Recover the gennaker.

Overtaking to windward on a run

Tactically you have the advantage, because your victim can't see you easily. Concentrate on boatspeed, luffing up and bearing away as appropriate. When you are approximately abeam of your rival choose an effective gust to bear away and drive over the top of him.

Overtaking to leeward on a run

The best option if you are running deeper and faster than your opponent is to gybe away into clear air, although this is not always an alternative. Breaking through a windward boat is difficult but not impossible - by working each gust more efficiently and using the apparent wind to sail deeper you can produce a sufficient gap to allow you to luff up at the opportune moment and drive through.

➡ In light winds or with a light crew you have to be more crafty. Secure the righting line to the crews' harness hook.

APPROACHING THE LEEWARD MARK

If you plan to approach on port, beware: half the fleet may be coming in starboard with an overlap on you, and you will have to give them room to go round inside. Try to keep good speed, aiming slightly above the buoy to allow for bearing away and dropping. As you bear away, the 'overlap line' swings in your favour.

If you are coming in on port and trying to get an overlap on the boat ahead you can consider a late drop, but if you reach the mark with your gennaker still half up you will be penalised if you force him to carry on or turn very wide.

Arriving at the leeward mark on starboard and planning to do a gybe drop is a good tactic because of the overlap (see above), but leave yourself a bit of room to turn and drop the gennaker. Once again, if you exit the mark

➡ Step onto the harness spreader bar.

● Stow it on the mast.

● Right the boat.

with the sail half down and can't come up to your proper course you could be penalised. My personal preference is to arrive near the mark on starboard and gybe about 20 lengths from it. This gives you the advantage of being on starboard for most of the way and also gives you time to do a clean gybe drop and make a smart rounding. There are laylines to the leeward mark and you need to think about where they are. Ideally you will gybe on the layline, but if you are in doubt and it's windy, gybe early to avoid having to reach to the mark. If it's light, you may choose to go past the layline, gybe late and come in to the mark higher on the wind with good apparent wind.

GUSTS AND TIDE

Gusts of wind travelling down the course are

your best opportunity for extra speed, more apparent wind and lower angles of sailing. By keeping an eye to windward you can detect which gusts are worth gybing back into.

Tides work for you by helping or hindering your progress, and also by moving the boat against the prevailing wind, increasing the apparent wind and the downwind sailing angles.

RECOVERING FROM A CAPSIZE

It's inadvisable to try and right the boat with the gennaker up because it'll be full of water and could immediately drag the boat back over again.

Basic recovery
Having capsized recover the crew, then position

● Turn......

● ....and exert maximum leverage.

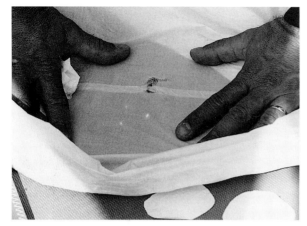

● Repairing a small hole.

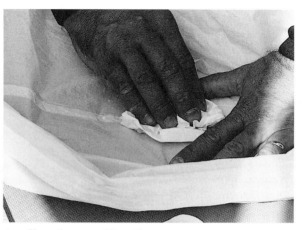

● Clean the area with meths.

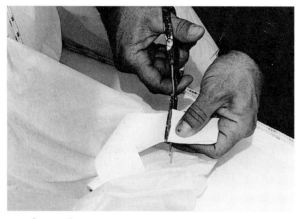

● Cut patches...

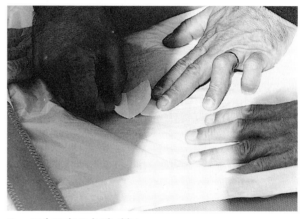

● and apply to both sides.

yourselves near the bow to act as a sea anchor: turning the boat so the sails point into the wind (see also page 69). One person now pulls down the gennaker either by pulling it into its chute or, if you have a bag, by bundling it so it rests on the side of the mast. Then prepare the sails and rudders as described on page 69 and right the boat. Once righted, hoist or fully recover the gennaker.

Recovery in light winds or when the crew is too light

To pull the boat up by conventional means recover the gennaker and prepare the boat as before.

Throw the righting line over the hull. One person hooks this to his trapeze harness and crouches down to let the second person step onto the spreader bar. The first person then swings out to a "trapezing position" and the two exert maximum leverage.

This is useful in light winds when there is not much help from the wind to lift the sail. There is very little weight on the trapezer because the other person is standing on the spreader bar and holding the righting line, but a little natural balance is required!

REPAIRING THE GENNAKER

You will inevitably rip the gennaker. Always carry a repair kit consisting of gennaker repair tape, cleaning fluid and scissors.

To repair the sail spread it out on a flat surface and clean both sides with meths (this also gets rid of any moisture). Cut two patches which are larger than the tear, and round the corners. Then stick them on both sides of the sail.

For small nicks, this will probably last for the life of the sail but for major damage you will need to replace it with a proper sailmaker's repair at a later date.

Advanced techniques

● Helming from the wire: try to sail low and fast.

HELMING FROM THE WIRE

As you move up to more powerful cats with bigger rigs you will need to have two people trapezing.

It's important that you feel comfortable on the wire and can control the boat from it.

Your first objectives are to be able to go out onto the wire smoothly, to be able to control the sheet and the tiller while you are out there and to be able to make a smooth transition back into the boat without stalling. When you can do all that, you're ready for tacking, gybing etc.

To go out
The problem is the tendency to pull the tiller as you go out which makes the boat bear away and pitches you forward, ie the opposite to what you're trying to do! Begin by sliding your hand out along the tiller extension behind your ear. The mainsheet is in the other hand, so when you go out you will automatically pull in

some sheet which will power up the rig and help balance your extra weight. Now hook on and roll out.

Trapezing from the wire
If it's windy you will want to be low as this is faster, but realistically you will have to be slightly higher than your crew so that you can see over him. You will be steering with the tiller in your back hand and the mainsheet in your front hand, but use the thumb of your tiller hand to hold excess sheet, probably coiled over the thumb.

To play the mainsheet you have several options.

For minor adjustments simply take two or three turns round your hand, then either pull in or let out as you wish.

Secondly, on a long beat get your crew to secure his jibsheet loosely, then pass him the mainsheet to play. This is particularly fast but requires good teamwork.

Alternatively, if you want to move large

⬥   Raise yourself a little so you can see over the crews body.

amounts of mainsheet yourself, you'll need to use your tiller hand as a clamp. Pull in with your mainsheet hand and bend the rope around the trapeze wire and clamp it in your tiller hand before changing grip with your mainsheet hand. Don't use the mainsheet jamming cleat as a temporary grip.

Coming back in

The natural tendency is to push the tiller as you come in, which simply turns the boat into the wind. Begin by moving your hand down on the shaft of the tiller extension. Now swing in,

either to sit on the side of the boat or use the trapeze handle to help you roll over your feet and finish up kneeling on the trampoline. This is very helpful if you then need to move about the boat or tack.

HOW THE HELMSMAN TACKS FROM THE WIRE

Your success here will depend on a combination of coming in and out smoothly, controlling the rudder, and powering up the rig at the right time on the new tack.

⬥   Tacking from the wire.   ⬥   Move in.   ⬥   Cross the boat.

♠ **Hold the tiller like this and use the thumb of your tiller hand to hold excess sheet.**

- Check the area to windward.
- Begin to turn the boat into the wind, and as she enters the no-go zone step into the boat.
- Release the trapeze wire using your mainsheet hand.
- Cross the boat on your knees, facing aft, changing tiller extension and mainsheet hands

in the process. You may need to ease some sheet in the middle of the tack, but this will be recovered as you roll out on the new side.
- Kneel on the windward hull with your feet over it. Hook on.
- Roll out, sheeting in the mainsail appropriately to power the boat off on the new tack.

Hook on.

Roll out.

Power off.

Tuning the mast

Mast tune is a 3-D puzzle. The mast can bend sideways, fore-and-aft or along its axis. Its shape and stability are determined by four main controls: diamond tension, downhaul tension, mast rotation and mainsheet tension. These four work through the sail and mast to increase or decrease the power.

The diamonds support about two-thirds of the mast. The rigidity of this part of the mast depends on the tension in the diamond wires, the length of the spreaders and the angle at which they sweep back.

So, for example, a light crew may need more pre-bend in strong winds and can achieve this by sweeping back the spreaders and increasing the tension in the diamond wires. In light winds they decrease the tension, and hence the pre-bend.

Note that sweeping back the spreaders or reducing diamond tension reduce the across-axis support to the mast, which may lead to loss of performance or even failure.

If in doubt tension up the diamond wires to create positive pre-bend. At a later stage you may choose to use a rig tension meter to obtain more accurate settings. For further information consult your class rigging manual.

Mainsail downhaul The effect of the downhaul dramatically changes the shape of the sail. By applying tension you attempt to shorten the luff length, compressing the mast and bending it across its axis from the top to the base. The effect is to flatten the sail and open the top third of the leech, an excellent tool for strong wind sailing. You need to practice using the downhaul effectively, smoothly and in coordination with the rest of the boat's equipment.

In one sense the downhaul is the fine tuning of the diamond rig settings, allowing you to increase and decrease power over a limited range. The job is normally carried out by the crew, easing the downhaul for power and applying tension when the boat feels over-powered or requires excessive amounts of mainsheet adjustment.

Mast rotation The initial purpose of allowing the mast to rotate is to give a smoother air flow over the leeward side of the sail.

Effectively this means pointing the leeward side towards the direction of the apparent wind. A second effect is mast bend. When downhaul or mainsheet tension is applied there is a pull down the luff or the leech. By adjusting rotation you increase or decrease the amount of bend in the top of the mast across the axis. By rotating the mast across the boat, leech or downhaul tension will bend the mast tip aft, and induce twist. By slowly de-rotating the mast towards fore-and-aft, the leech is hardened up, giving less twist and a flatter sail.

A good basic rule is to point the spanner bar towards the shroud plate for light and medium winds, moving it towards the rear beam housing as the wind increases.

But note that too much de-rotation will result in the top of the mast bending off to leeward, giving reduced performance.

Mainsheet tension The mainsheet also controls sail twist and the bend in the mast tip. Increasing mainsheet tension reduces twist, but the resulting leech tension can also bend the tip of the mast aft, the exact amount depending on mast rotation.

The mainsail clew outhaul affects the low part of the sail: pull it on fully for beating, have a medium setting for reaching and let it off for running.

To really understand your rig you need to spend time watching and feeling it react. This is best done on the shore with the boat secured, on the water from a support boat and through sailing.

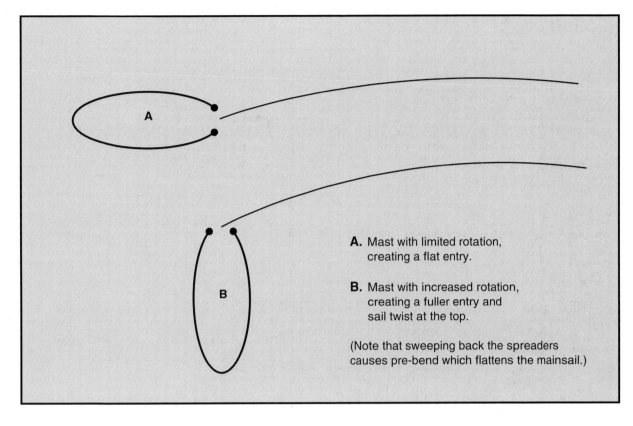

A. Mast with limited rotation, creating a flat entry.

B. Mast with increased rotation, creating a fuller entry and sail twist at the top.

(Note that sweeping back the spreaders causes pre-bend which flattens the mainsail.)

TROUBLESHOOTING

Sailing scenario 1 - Light sailors are overpowered to windward.
Firstly, pull on more downhaul. If this is insufficient then increase the pre-bend by cranking up on the diamond wires. This gives permanent de-powering.

Sailing scenario 2 - We can't point.
You are either pinching or haven't enough power in the rig.

To put more permanent power back into the rig ease the downhaul and/or reduce pre-bend and increase mast rotation. Note that easing the mainsheet can help too as it does virtually the same job as the downhaul in certain conditions.

SUMMING UP

A high performance catamaran requires a team to make it work. The helm and crew need to be working together to keep the boat up to maximum speed.

Big rigs and extra sails are an advantage in light winds, but the key to successful high performance cat sailing lies in a good under-standing of how to control them as the wind increases. I hope this book has given you that understanding and that you enjoy your catamaran sailing as much as I have.

Good luck from myself and the Cat. Clinic team. We look forward to seeing you on the water!

Fernhurst Books is the leading nautical publisher.

For a free full-colour brochure phone,
fax or write to us at:

Fernhurst Books,
Duke's Path, High Street, Arundel,
West Sussex, BN18 9AJ.

Phone: 01903 882277
Fax: 01903 882715
Email: sales@fernhurstbooks.co.uk